FIFTY CURIOUS QUESTIONS

PABULUM FOR THE ENQUIRING MIND

MARTIN FONE

authorHOUSE®

AuthorHouse™ UK
1663 Liberty Drive
Bloomington, IN 47403 USA
www.authorhouse.co.uk
Phone: 0800.197.4150

Published by AuthorHouse 07/24/2017

ISBN: 978-1-5462-8002-6 (sc)
ISBN: 978-1-5462-8003-3 (hc)
ISBN: 978-1-5462-8001-9 (e)

CONTENTS

This book is dedicated to my parents, Ray and
Brenda, who fostered my enquiring mind.

INTRODUCTION

The pace of life is such that we rarely have the luxury to stop and think. We take so much on trust. We assume that we know why something happens or the way things work. It is only when we stop and think that nagging doubts or questions creep into our subconscious. For those of us blessed – or is it cursed? – with an enquiring mind, once the seed of a question has been planted, we need to find the answer.

The purpose of this book is to shed light on some of those nagging and irritating questions. There is no overarching design behind the fifty questions. They are just some of the topics that have puzzled me (a self-confessed ignoramus on all matters scientific) over the years, and I have now had the time to find the answers. Fortunately, greater brains than mine have grappled with some of the issues and carried out bizarre experiments or made quantum leaps of logic to push out further the frontiers of human knowledge. This book celebrates this quest and thirst for knowledge.

In these pages we will explore how our body works: why we blush, why we feel colder when we step out of the shower, and whether there is a finite limit to how long our hair will grow. We will perfect some essential life skills such as how to spot a liar, handle a hangover, rid ourselves of hiccups, and construct the perfect cream scone. There are some deep existential questions to answer, like how long is a generation and whether we are only six feet away from a rat. And then there are some really maddening questions like, Why do we still use a QWERTY keyboard? and Why do the British persist in driving on the left hand side of the road? All will be revealed inside these pages.

We also consider some left-field questions like: Do we lose weight when we fart? Do elephants take longer to urinate than horses? and When you are caught in the rain, do you get wetter if you run or walk to your destination? Life would be all the poorer without the answers to questions like these.

I hope you enjoy reading this book as much as I have putting it together. Many of the articles are based on posts that appeared on my eclectic blog windowthroughtime.wordpress.com – Check it out.

Finally, this book would not have been possible without the love and support of my wonderful wife, Jenny aka TOWT (The One-Woman Tsunami, an elemental force of nature). I am eternally in her debt.

Do you lose weight when you fart?

'Fart proudly', proclaimed Benjamin Franklin in 1781, and who am I to argue? It is a natural bodily function, and all you need are intestines and an anus. So yes, even the fairer sex breaks wind. The main carbohydrate responsible for flatulence is raffinose, a sugar commonly found in vegetables such as cabbage and broccoli and which our guts find hard to digest.

When I started thinking about farts, I soon realised there was much I didn't know about the subject. After all, if the principal constituents of a fart are nitrogen, hydrogen, carbon dioxide, oxygen, and methane – the smelly component is the 1 per cent of hydrogen sulphide – gasses all, and gasses have mass, what is the volume of an average fart, and has anybody bothered to find out? Upon doing some diligent research in the nether regions of the Internet, I struck gold, and I think the results are worth repeating.

I found a reference to an article in the ever popular journal *Gut*, which described the experiments of gastroenterologists from the Human Gastrointestinal Physiology and Nutrition Department of Sheffield's Royal Hallamshire hospital in 1991. They took ten volunteers and fed them with 200 grams of baked beans in addition to their normal diet. The volunteers' flatulence was collected via rectal catheters, and to ensure that there was an air-tight seal between the catheter and their bottoms, they were required to sit in a bath of water whilst passing wind.

Methodology having been established, we pass on to results. Our researchers found that the amount of gas produced over a twenty-four-hour period varied widely: between 476 and 1491 millilitres, with a median result of 705. There was no variation between the sexes in the amount passed, and farting tended to be more robust after eating. A single fart, regardless of sex, body size, or time of day, has a volume of between 33 and 125 millilitres, with a median of 90. Incidentally, although not part of this experiment, a fart has been recorded as reaching a speed of ten feet per second. The study found that those on a low-fibre diet reduced most of the fermentation gases that would have been expelled, and their average flatulence volume was a paltry 200 millilitres.

For the enquiring mind, this raises a further question, which the Sheffield researchers did not address: Do you lose weight after a fart? I regret to say, I have failed to find a definitive answer to that question. There was a post on Facebook, a most unreliable source of information in my experience, suggesting that you burn 67 calories per fart. For those who think I may have uncovered the perfect form of weight loss, the website Fat Loss School is ready to pour a bucket of cold water over the idea. They claim that when you fart, the muscles relax and the pressure in your bowels does all the work in expelling the gas. The only way you would achieve a measurable figure in the calories burned whilst farting would be by straining yourself to the limit.

So now we know!

Why is the penis on an ancient Greek statue so small?

In the days before the Internet and when pornography was a top-shelf affair, one way that was open to appreciate the human form in all its glory was to pore over dusty volumes of Greek and Roman statuary. The fact you were mugging up on classical civilization gave your prurient interest a patina of respectability. But to an adolescent with an enquiring mind, the exercise could raise more questions than it answered, particularly, Why are the penises that have survived the ravages of time so small? And why do the statues exhibit remarkable scrotal asymmetry? Fortunately, help was at hand.

Starting with the penis, the ancient Greeks weren't as obsessed with size as we seem to be these days. Where statues exist with large penises, they are usually of grotesque characters such as satyrs or the god Priapus, who was cursed by Hera with a permanent erection, impotence, and ugliness and was ejected from Olympus. Large penises were associated with qualities such as foolishness, lust, and ugliness, which are not the sort of attributes you want to endow your gods and heroes with. A small penis, on the other hand, was a sign of rationality and that your appendage was in proportion with the rest of your body. It was the epitome of the perfect male form.

The comedian Aristophanes, as often was the case, was the man to go to for confirmation of this view. He wrote in *The Clouds*: 'If you do these things, I tell you, and bend your efforts to them, you will always have a shining breast, a bright skin, big shoulders, a minute tongue, a big rump and a small prick'. It was not the size, it seemed, it was what you did with it that counted.

In 2012 a survey conducted by Dr Richard Lynn, emeritus professor of psychology at Ulster University, into the penis sizes of representatives of 116 countries, revealed that the Koreans (North and South) had the smallest penises (at 3.8 inches), whereas the largest were those from the Republic of Congo (at 7.06 inches). The British member stood proudly at number seventy-nine, at 5.5 inches.

I remember, when I went to be measured for my first bespoke suit, being flummoxed by the Mr Humphries of the town, enquiring how I dressed and realising that 'underpants, shirt, then trousers' was not the answer he was looking for. In 1960, K S F Chang revealed that in right-handed men the right testis tended to be higher than the left whereas in left-handed men it was the left that was the higher of the two.

Like any man with an enquiring mind, he wondered whether this was anything to do with weight, in other words: In right-handed men, was the left testis the heavier? An empirical approach was adopted, and the testes of cadavers were measured for weight and volume. The results were surprising. In right-handed men, the right testis, the higher of the two, was the heavier and of greater volume than the left. So even though it hung higher, it was the heavier. For those who are wondering, the respective weights are 9.95 and 9.36 grams and volumes 9.69 and 9.10 cubic centimetres.

As far back as 1764, the aptly named J J Winckelmann noted testicular asymmetry in Greek and Roman statues, reporting 'the left testicle is always the larger, as it is in nature'. In a well-balanced survey reported in *Nature* in 1976, Chris McManus observed the scrotal asymmetry of 107 sculptures of antique origin or Renaissance copies and found that in the largest group, the right testicle was placed higher, but the left is larger. And in the second largest group, the left is the higher, but the right the larger. The artists had made the same error as Winckelmann, probably assuming that the lower hanging testis must be the heavier.

So now we know!

Why doesn't glue stick in the tube?

One of the benefits of being pig ignorant of the physical laws that govern our universe is that the answer to mundane questions such as this can elicit a sense of wonderment. When I understand what is going on, I get that feeling of contentment that the likes of Isaac Newton and Albert Einstein must have had when they had cracked a particularly thorny problem.

The solution to the glue question is all to do with water and something called *mechanical adhesion*. Ordinary glue – we will come on to superglue in a minute – is made up of a variety of polymers, long strands that are either stretchy or sticky. The key to good glue is finding the optimal combination of sticky and stretchy polymers.

Anyway, ordinary glue contains water, and it is this that acts as a solvent that keeps the glue liquid until you want to use it. When you apply the glue to a piece of paper, for example, the water is exposed to air and eventually evaporates. The process of evaporation causes the glue to dry and harden, leaving only the sticky polymers to do their job – to adhere to the surface.

OK, that makes sense. But why doesn't this process of mechanical adhesion occur when the glue is in the tube? It is all down to the amount of air that is present in the tube. In a tube with the top firmly in place, there is insufficient air present to cause the water in the glue to evaporate. So the glue remains in a liquid form and not so sticky as to stick to the insides of the tube. If, however, you forget to put the top back on or don't screw it tightly enough, you will find that the contents will dry up.

Superglue is another kettle of fish, though, being made up of a chemical called cyanoacrylate instead of polymers. This works through chemical adhesion. The reaction of the cyanoacrylate with the water vapour in the air causes the glue to bond. As there is always water vapour present in the air, no matter how dry it may seem to you, superglue reacts more quickly and is more prone to dry out in poorly sealed containers. This chemical adhesion explains why I always get into an unholy mess when I use superglue – it gets everywhere and sticks to everything before I even get it to where I intend to apply it – and why ordinary glue seems easier to apply.

So the answer is water, but with ordinary glue you need to keep the H_2O in the tube to prevent it from drying out and becoming sticky whereas with superglue you need to keep the water out to stop the substance from hardening.

Isn't science wonderful?

Whilst we are on the subject of tubes, what gets my goat is my inability to wring the last drops of whatever is in it out of its container. This inherent design flaw increases the manufacturer's profit. As we still live in times of austerity, here's a handy tip that is guaranteed to solve the problem. When you have reached maximum frustration point with the tube, simply snip off the top or bottom (or both) of the tube and access the contents that way. When you've finished, use a clothes peg or a food tie to seal it up again. Of course, for the reasons discussed above, this may not be terribly effective with glue, but it works a treat with toothpaste!

Every little helps!

Are bees really busy?

By the time I left university, I was heartily sick of bees. I had studied Vergil's fourth book of the *Georgics* at both A level and degree level and could pretty much tell you everything the poet knew about the blessed pollinators. Not that I have anything against them per se – and in our garden we cultivate plants especially to attract them – but at the time, enough was enough.

Vergil's thesis was that bees are like human society. They work, are devoted to a king (or a queen in the case of bees) and are willing to die for a cause. Over the millennia they have gained a reputation for being industrious. 'As busy as a bee' is a popular idiom still in vogue. But is this reputation well-deserved?

Where bees forage, workers can make up to one hundred foraging trips a day, but their activities cease at sundown. Other bees, whose responsibilities include tending the honeycombs and cooling the nest, work around the clock but also take frequent breaks. Drones, on the other hand, don't leave the hive until early afternoon and rely on other bees to feed them.

Research conducted by the University of Illinois sheds some light on how busy bees are. Five honeybee colonies were used in the experiments – three in natural outdoor areas and the other two in special screened enclosures. Each hive was equipped with pairs of laser scanners at the entrances and between one and three hundred workers from each colony were tagged with tiny micro-transponders which enabled the scanners to tag their IDs, direction of travel, and time of day.

After a couple of months' data gathering, the scientists saw that a small proportion of the bees, around 20 per cent, were much busier than the rest, accounting for up to 50 per cent of all the recorded flight activity. These busy bees began making flights as soon as the colony became active each morning and made regular, closely spaced flights throughout the day until the colony called a halt to its flight activities in the evening.

These busy bees, though, weren't always busy, and the levels of their activity peaked and troughed over the course of the experiment and their lifetimes. This observation encouraged the scientists to wonder whether their industriousness was an adaptive response rather than an innate one. In other words, did the bees adapt their work patterns to prevailing conditions, and would those bees that were less energetic mend their ways in the absence of the busy bees?

Cunningly, the researchers lurked at the entrances to the enclosed hives at peak foraging time and captured all the bees that arrived there. When they looked at the flight records of the bees they had captured, the majority were in the top 20 per cent of the workforce.

For the rest of that day, activity at the feeders was quiet, but the following day, it had resumed at normal levels. Some of the bees that had been taking it easy because of the endeavours of the busy bees upped their activity levels by up to 500 per cent. The scientists concluded that there isn't a sharp divide in the hive between workers and slackers but that each worker keeps a check on the overall activity of the colony and adjusts its own endeavours to ensure that the overall needs of the colony are met.

Perhaps Vergil's simile that bees reflect human society is more spot on than I thought. Bees aren't busy per se but, like humans, do enough to get by.

So now we know!

Why do we still use the QWERTY keyboard?

I'm not the greatest of typists; I'm very much of the two-stubby-finger variety. In addition to my poor digital dexterity, I put it down to the layout of the keyboard. Who came up with it, and why do we persist in using it?

The first practical typewriter was developed as long ago as 1868 and patented in the US by Christopher Latham Scholes. It had a moveable carriage, a lever for turning paper from line to line, and a keyboard which was laid out in alphabetical order. However, there was a fundamental problem with the layout of the keyboard: when typists worked quickly and used keys that were adjacent to each other, the keys kept jamming. This meant that the typist had to stop to free the keys. Worse still, the keys on the earliest typewriters struck the back of the paper, and so mistakes became apparent only when the paper was removed from the machine.

Scholes scratched his head, realized he was unable to solve the problem of the sticking keys, and concocted a Plan B – a disposition of the characters in a way that would slow the typist down. After much experimentation and using a study of letter-pair frequency prepared by the brother of Scholes's principal financial backer, Amos Densmore, he settled on the QWERTY arrangement. He considered the new arrangement important enough to include it in his next patent application in 1878.

Scholes went into PR overdrive, claiming that the new keyboard's arrangement of letters was scientific and would boost speed and efficiency. The reality was anything but. The most accessible row of the typewriter keyboard is the middle one. Although about 70 per cent of words in English can be typed using the letters A, D, E, H, I, N, O, R S, and T, only

A appears on the middle row. Only about three hundred English words can be typed using the right hand alone whereas around three thousand can be typed using just the left. As most people are right-handed, the keyboard layout favours our left-handed brethren. At the very least, the hands have to travel further over the keyboard than would have been the case with an alphabetic layout.

For office technology at the time, the advantages of having a typewriter outweighed the disadvantages in terms of speed and efficiency that the QWERTY keyboard imposed, and so typists learned the new layout and got on with it.

There have been attempts to (re)introduce a more logical keyboard arrangement. The most successful was the Dvorak Simplified Keyboard (DSK), developed and patented by August Dvorak, cousin of the Czech composer, and revealed to an unreceptive world in 1932. Dvorak had been inspired by the work of Frank and Lillian Gilbreth, pioneers in the field of workplace efficiency. Unfortunately, it never caught on although on modern computer keyboards, you can find the layout as an option buried deep in the software settings.

It seems strange that we have continued to use a solution to a technological deficiency of the earliest typewriters, particularly as most of us now pound away on keyboards that don't have keys that have to make an impression on a piece of paper. This is clearly an interesting example of how we have adapted to technological deficiencies rather than changing the technology.

Is celebratory gunfire dangerous?

I have never understood the fascination with firearms. And I have always thought the bizarre practice of firing live ammunition above your head is intensely dangerous. (You must have seen footage of soldiers firing off to celebrate some victory.)

Casualties have been recorded from celebratory gunfire. For example, in Turkey in 2010, a bridegroom killed three of his relatives when he fired off an AK-47 at his wedding. And in the Philippines in 2011, three were killed by stray bullets during a New Year's celebration. In Minnesota, I'm told, it is illegal to fire bullets up in the air in a cemetery.

Since what goes up must come down, it is natural for the enquiring mind to wonder just how lethal the practice is. The starting point would seem to be to establish the speed at which a bullet needs to be travelling in order to penetrate the human skin. You would have thought that with the billions invested in developing weaponry and the centuries of practice in firing bullets either in anger or at targets such as pig carcasses and ballistic gel, this would seem to be a piece of knowledge honed to fine precision. But apparently not.

The best I can find is an estimate put forward by those shadowy characters, munitions experts. They estimate that a bullet must be travelling at a speed of at least two hundred feet a second in order to break the skin. However, there are circumstances in which a bullet travelling as fast as 330 feet per second might just bounce off your body. Two factors that can impact how lethal the shot is are how pointed the bullet is and what part of your body it strikes. Skin thickness varies between individuals and in different parts of the body. The skin in the upper lip, for example, is 50 per cent thicker than that on the chin. And inevitably, age is a factor. The skin of babies is thin and the skin of the elderly less elastic, meaning that bullets can penetrate it more easily.

A gunshot fired straight up into the sky can reach a height of ten thousand feet, and its speed and direction are prone to be affected by prevailing winds. Consider, too, the point at which air resistance balances the accelerating force of gravity, known as terminal velocity. For a .30-calibre rifle, this is around three hundred feet per second, and for bullets from something like a nine-millimetre handgun, it is a paltry 150 to 200 feet per second. Bear in mind, though, that air resistance decreases at altitude, so it is intuitively more dangerous to fire a gun to celebrate climbing Everest.

Then, of course, we have the angle at which the bullet is fired. The general consensus seems to be that if the bullet is fired vertically, at ninety degrees to the ground, it is unlikely to be lethal. This is because on the way down, air resistance will prevent the bullet from maintaining its initial velocity. It may give you a painful shock, but unless you are hit directly in (say) the eye or mouth, you are likely to come out of the experience intact. And bullets fired vertically generally fall with the pointed end upwards or at least sideways.

And this is pretty much the case until you get to an angle of forty-five degrees where the actions of air resistance and gravity have less of an effect on moderating the bullet's initial velocity.

So now we know. I still think it is safer to pop a champagne cork.

Are we really never more than six feet away from a rat?

Having spent most of my working life in the city of London, I can well believe it, but if we are talking about Rattus norvegicus, I have never been convinced. I can count the number of times I have seen a real live rat on my fingers and toes and perhaps have one or two left over. What I do know is that they are no respecter of surroundings. I have seen one in a so-called luxury hotel, scuttling across the bar area, to the consternation of some and the amusement of the other guests. I've seen others, as you might expect, rummaging around rubbish piles. Normally, they are shy creatures and go out of their way to avoid humans.

It is difficult to know how this canard has come about. One finger of suspicion has been pointed at W R Boetler, who, in his 1909 blockbuster, *The Rat Problem*, tried to establish whether it was reasonable to suppose that there was one rat for every acre of cultivated land in the UK. He was reduced to making an educated guess. As there were forty million acres of farmland at the time and a UK population of forty million, the conclusion that there was one rat for every one of us was too tempting to resist.

Let's look at the problem another way. If we assume that a rat has a circular area to itself, then in order for it to never be more than six feet away from where we happen to be, the circular area it will occupy will be some 11.49 square metres. The UK occupies some 245 billion square metres, so for rats to be evenly distributed in their 11.49 square metre areas, there would have to be some 21.3 billion of them. This seems highly unlikely.

Fortunately, Dr Dave Cowan of the Food and Environment Research Agency can provide us with some assistance. The first thing is to know something about rats. The particular nugget of wisdom that helps is that they are completely commensal here in Blighty. In other words, they have a symbiotic relationship with humans.

There are four places where rats may be found: in and around our houses, in commercial premises, down sewers, and on agricultural premises. We can now do the maths.

It is rare for rats to live in our houses – around 0.5 per cent are infested – but they are more common outside in gardens, compost heaps, and outbuildings. Even so, only 3 per cent of premises have a problem with rats, and where they are, there are relatively few of them. Cowan calculated the number of domestic rats at around 1.5 million. Five per cent of the 1.8 million commercial premises have rats in residence, a measly total of around 200,000. There are around 16 thousand square kilometres of sewers in the UK, of which around 5 per cent have rats. In the 1950s, a survey was conducted into the number of rats in sewers, and a figure of 2,000 per square kilometre was arrived at. This means that there are some 1.6 million down the sewers, making a total of around 3 to 3.5 million in urban environments.

If we move to the country, the picture is somewhat different. Around 40 per cent of the 200,000 agricultural premises in the UK have rats, and on average there are 90 rats on a farm. Multiplying it all gives us some 7 million rural rats and some 10.5 million rats overall.

The UK has around 16,000 square kilometres of urban space. So if all the urban rats were distributed evenly, each one would have 5,000 square metres to roam around. If you were standing in any one spot in an urban environment, at worst you would be some 50 metres away from a rat.

Has anyone calibrated the intensity of insect stings?

A little while ago, I was stung by a wasp. The pesky creature somehow managed to work its way through the vent in my shirtsleeve and then got itself stuck. As I might have done in similar circumstances, the wasp panicked, and in its anxiety to find a way out, it stung me. Jolly painful it was too. I managed to realise what was going on before it had chance to strike again and, I regret, in an uncharacteristic lapse into an un-Zen-like state, I killed it.

It was a surprise to me to learn that there is such a thing as the Schmidt sting pain index, which rates, using the honeybee as a reference point, the painfulness of a sting from one of seventy-eight carefully selected species of Hymenoptera – bees, ants, wasps, and the like to you and me. Schmidt worked out a scale running from zero to four, nought being awarded to a creature that packs a sting that isn't capable of breaking the skin, and a massive four, as they say on game shows, to the most painful stings known. Only the bullet ant and the tarantula hawk scored a perfect four. Forearmed is forewarned, they say.

That's all very well and useful for consoling yourself that your temporary pain could have been so much worse if you had encountered a bullet ant in full flow, but, as Michael L Smith of Cornell University realised, that is only half the story. Surely the sensation of pain will vary depending upon where in the body you are stung. If that is true, there can be no absolute value allocated to the sting of any one of the Hymenoptera family. So, as is the way with scientists, he decided to conduct an experiment to establish whether and how pain varies depending on sting location.

The way he chose to experiment was to take the humble honeybee – or a number of them, I would imagine – and get them to sting one of twenty five selected body parts. Research thrives on volunteers willing to help the people in white coats extend the limits of human knowledge, but for some unaccountable reason, Smith couldn't find any and so conducted the experiments on himself.

If I remember my chemistry, you need to describe your methodology when recounting an experiment, and Smith's was fairly simple. He held the bee against the part of the body to be tested until the sting was first felt; kept it there for five seconds; then pulled the bee away, leaving the stinger in place for one minute before removing it with tweezers. Of course, by this time the honeybee is dead. Smith devised a scale running from one to ten to determine or describe the intensity of the pain in any given body part, and each part was stung three times. The pain rating for each location was averaged over the three rounds and ranked according to score. As Smith drily observed in his paper: 'All the stings induced pain in the author'.

The clear message from this research is that pain really does vary according to where you are stung. The lowest-ranked places were the skull, middle toe, and upper arm, all scoring 2.3, whereas the most painful parts were the nostril (scoring 9.0), the upper lip (8.7), and the penis shaft (7.3). Armpit, cheek, palm and scrotum all scored 7.0. If you are looking to enjoy a 5.0, then you need to be stung on the foot arch, forearm, or back of the knee.

This is really handy to know, but we are reliant upon Smith's pain threshold being roughly in line with our own. I think we need more data. Any volunteers?

How do you take a group photo without anyone blinking?

It is a truth universally acknowledged that whenever a group photograph is taken, there is always at least someone who manages to be snapped with closed eyes. Blinking is a natural eye function that spreads tears across and removes irritants from the surface of the cornea and conjunctiva. For the perfectionists amongst us and for those with an enquiring mind, the obvious questions are: Is it possible to get a group photo without someone blinking in it? and How many shots will you need to take to be sure you have one picture with everyone wide-eyed?

The trite answer is just one, provided you give each of the subjects a pair of matchsticks to prop their peepers open. However, if you want a natural photo, or at least as natural as a group photo is ever likely to be, then you need to resort to some mathematics and probability theory. Fortunately, someone cleverer than I has cracked his grey cells to shed some light on this First–World problem. Step forward, Dr Piers Barnes, a physicist from the Commonwealth Scientific and Industrial Research Organisation.

The starting point is the blink. The average number of times a person blinks when being photographed is ten, and an average blink lasts 250 milliseconds. Unlike yawning, where one person can trigger a spate of copycat yawns amongst bystanders, there is no evidence that one person blinking influences another. Each blink is an independent event, and when we have a group of people, each of their blinks will be independent of all the others'. The only occasions when this might not be the case is if the group are standing in something like a sandstorm, but let's ignore this unnecessary complication. Each blink will also be random. They won't all occur uniformly every six seconds.

In good indoor light, the shutter of a camera stays open for eight milliseconds, a period of time considerably shorter than the duration of a blink. So from a probability theory perspective, the chance of someone blinking while a photo is being taken is the expected number of blinks, which we will call x, multiplied by the period of time (t) during which the photo could be spoilt. The reciprocal, $1 / xt$, is the probability of one person not blinking while a photo is being taken.

Following this logic through, if you have a group of people posing for a photograph (we denote the number by the symbol n), then the probability of a good group photo with no one blinking would be $(1 - xt)^n$, and the number of photos required to get the perfect shot will be $1 / (1 - xt)^n$. With me so far?

Plotting the formula on a graph shows a normal distribution, which will enable you to calculate the number of shots you would need to guarantee, at least statistically speaking, a perfect photo for any size of group. What it does mean is that if there is a group of fifty or more, there is virtually no chance of an unspoilt photo. Remember that when you are planning your wedding photo list.

Of course, in the heat of the moment, even the brainiest of photographers might not be able to make the necessary calculations. Helpfully, Barnes has developed a rule of thumb for calculating the number of shots for groups of under twenty people. In good light, divide the number of people by three, and in poor light use two as the denominator.

So now we know. Happy snapping!

Do elephants take longer to urinate than horses?

When I was a young schoolboy, I well remember a teacher, when describing Roman religious practices, coming up with the killer line that he had never seen an auspice. How we all roared! Now that I am a mature adult, I have seen a horse piss, and a prodigious quantity of steaming urine they produce, to be sure. I have also had the privilege of watching many other species of the animal kingdom passing water. I don't know if it is just serendipity or whether the sight of me causes them to micturate.

Anyway, I have long wondered whether it takes a creature the size of an elephant longer to urinate than a horse, for example. I find questions of this sort nag away at me. This book is intended to answer them.

Help is at hand from some research conducted at Zoo Atlanta in Georgia and published in the ever popular Proceedings of the National Academy of Science. These researchers thought that because large creatures such as rhinos have bigger bladders than dogs, they therefore take longer to go about their business. They set out to prove this by installing high-speed cameras to capture their performance. Thirty-two species, ranging in size from a mouse to an elephant, and including jaguars and gorillas, were tested.

The findings were fascinating. It wasn't the size of the animal's bladder that was the key determinant but their overall size. The tipping point for mammals is a weight of 6 lbs. Despite an elephant's bladder capacity of eighteen litres compared with a cat's of five millilitres, all mammals with a weight in excess of six pounds urinated on average for twenty-one seconds, give or take.

It is all down to flow rates, apparently. An elephant can urinate faster than a cat because its urethra is wider and longer, allowing the force of gravity to act more strongly on fluid flowing through it. Creatures with weights below six pounds, on the other hand, have urinary tracts that are so small that they have to battle against capillary action – a tendency for the urine's molecules to stick to themselves and the walls of their tracts and flow back up again. Instead of producing a stream of urine, their pee is so viscous and moves so slowly that it falls out in droplets.

Fascinating stuff, and useful too. If you are unfortunate enough to be stuck in a shower of elephant urine, at least you now know that your ordeal will last around twenty-one seconds. Makes it seem almost bearable!

So now we know!

How much does a soul weigh?

As I get older, I am increasingly drawn to wonder about metempsychosis – the transmigration of the soul. There is at odd moments something vaguely comforting to think that as I draw my last breath, my essence will zip away to somewhere better. The Orphics, after all, believed that the soul and the body are bound together by a rather uncomfortable agreement: The soul, being divine and immortal, forever aspires to freedom; whereas the body holds it as a prisoner in chains. Upon death the soul is released only to be imprisoned once more as the cycle of life begins again. On the other hand, I remember Hilary Mantel's disconcerting observation in *Beyond Black* that spirits retain the characteristics of their owners. No one would want to get stuck with some obnoxious so-and-sos for eternity.

Greater minds than mine have pondered, generally from a philosophical standpoint, whether there is such a thing as a soul. I do not intend to discuss here the arguments for and against (you will be relieved to read), but I was attracted by the empirical approach adopted in 1901 by an American physician, Dr Duncan MacDougall. He reasoned that the only way to demonstrate conclusively whether an entity has a soul is to weigh it immediately prior to death and then immediately after death.

His guinea pigs were six patients in a home for the elderly who were hours away from dying from tuberculosis. Each patient (on a bed) was placed on an industrial-sized scale, which MacDougall claimed to be sensitive to within a fifth of an ounce. When they had taken their final breath, they were popped on the scales again. The first old codger who was subjected to this rather undignified experiment recorded a weight loss of twenty-one grams upon death. Ergo this was the weight of the soul.

MacDougall also turned his attention to dogs, weighing them fifteen minutes immediately before and after death. (There are suggestions that he might have killed them during his experiments.) In each case there was no discernible variation in weight. Rather than casting doubts on his methodology, MacDougall concluded that dogs don't have souls.

The *New York Times* ran a story on 11 March 1907, describing his experiments and findings under the wonderful headline 'Soul has weight, doctor thinks'. The results were published in the *Journal of the American Society for Psychical Research* the following month and were also reported in the journal *American Medicine*.

MacDougall's problems started as soon as these remarkable findings were published. A fellow physician, Augustus P Clarke, commented that at the time of death, because the lungs are no longer cooling the blood, there is an increase in sweating, which in itself could directly cause the loss of weight. Dogs, on the other hand, had no sweat glands, and the body would not lose weight from excessive sweating at the point of death. This would explain why the mutts' weight stayed stable.

Worse was to come. Another critic pointed out that MacDougall had been highly selective in his use of data. Only one old codger lost weight, one lost weight and then promptly put it back on, another two lost weight and then some time after death lost even more, and two results could not be obtained because of technical difficulties. In other words, the twenty-one grams was the only reading out of six that supported MacDougall's hypothesis and so the findings had no scientific merit.

MacDougall had the last laugh, though, as twenty-one grams has stuck in the popular psyche as the weight of a soul. But whether there is a soul is anybody's guess.

?

Do you get wetter running or walking in the rain?

I'm sure you've been there too. You are out for a walk without a jacket or an umbrella, and what was a bright blue sky when you set out suddenly turns grey. It starts to rain. What to do? You either run to the nearest shelter and wait until the shower passes over, or you carry on, curse your stupidity for not bringing an umbrella, and get wet. An everyday scenario for sure, but for the enquiring mind, it poses a very real question: Do you get wetter if you run or walk in the rain?

Naturally, greater brains than mine have pondered this question. Two obvious approaches can be adopted to derive the truth: the empirical and the abstract. Let's deal with the empirical first.

I am indebted to the ever popular journal *Health* for this account of an experiment conducted by Thomas Peterson and Trevor Wallis, two members of the National Climatic Data Center in the United States. Naturally, they required a rainy day to conduct their experiment. When conditions were judged to be ideal, they put on identical track suits and hats. To prevent their underwear from absorbing any of the rainwater and thereby invalidating the results, they wore plastic rubbish bags underneath their trackies. Having identified earlier a suitable hundred-metre course, they set off, Peterson walking and Wallis running.

Once they had completed their course and had got back into the dry, they removed their outer clothing and weighed it. Peterson's clothing had absorbed 7.5 ounces of water whereas Wallis's had sucked up just 4.5

ounces. The obvious conclusion from the empiricists was that you get wetter walking in the rain than running.

And now to the more rigorous scientific approach. The bellwether for the algebraic approach to answering our poser is Harvard mathematician David E Bell, who published what many consider to be the definitive analysis in the *Mathematical Gazette* in 1976. He developed an algebraic formula, fearsome to the untrained eye, which (if I am correct in my interpretation) suggests that if the rain is falling vertically or the wind is blowing in your face, you should run. Indeed, the faster you run, the less wet you will be over a defined distance. If the wind is blowing from behind you, the optimal speed at which you should run to minimise how wet you get is the speed of the wind.

In case you think that you need to emulate Usain Bolt to reduce the extent of your soaking, Bell's formula suggests that running at what would be an Olympic record-breaking pace (making no allowance for the use of illegal stimulants) would reduce your soaking by only 10 per cent.

Of course, as long as there is a problem, people will always take contrary stances. Alessandro de Angelis, a physicist at the University of Udine in Italy, espoused an alternative interpretation in an article in *Discovery* magazine. Although my research has failed to unearth the formula he used, he calculated that when you compare a sprinter who runs at 22.4 miles per hour with a walker who goes at 6.7 miles an hour – a cracking pace, in my view – the sprinter will be only 10 per cent drier. Ergo running isn't worth the bother.

This is a conclusion I have a lot of empathy for as any form of energetic exercise is anathema to me. So next time I'm out and get caught by a shower, I shall just curse my stupidity for forgetting my umbrella and carry on my merry way. I'm going to get wet whether I run or walk, and to reduce the degree of my soaking by expending unnecessary energy just doesn't seem worth it.

Can hallucinogens create religious ecstasy?

Ever since I saw a sadhu in India, I have wondered whether there is a correlation between religious ecstasy and drugs. Could the use of hallucinogens in a religious context produce the sort of mystical sensations that some religious devotees claim to have had? It seems I am not the only one to have pondered the question, as evidenced by a bizarre experiment conducted by one Walter Pahnke, working alongside LSD advocate Timothy Leary, on Good Friday of 1962 at the Marsh Chapel at Boston University.

Twenty students were asked to meet in the crypt of the chapel two hours before the service. They were put into groups of four, two of each group being given capsules containing psilocybin (aka magic mushroom powder) and the other two, perhaps disappointingly, received placebos. The placebo, however, contained 200 milligrams of niacin, a vitamin that produces hot flushes, simulating some of the symptoms of the mushrooms. Each group of four was chaperoned by two minders.

The guinea pigs were then led into a small chapel in the crypt where a service conducted by Pastor Howard Thurman, including a sermon, was piped to them through a loudspeaker. As the service progressed, ten of the students – the ones who had taken the placebo – sat attentively. The behaviour of the other ten was eccentric and more interesting.

Some wandered around the chapel, muttering to themselves; one sprawled across a pew; and another lay down on the floor. One enterprising student sat down at the organ and played a series of what were described as dissonant chords. Another was so taken by Thurman's call to spread the word that he rushed out into the street and had to be hauled back. Another had to be given an antidote.

Five of the minders had also been given psilocybin and behaved oddly. Even by five o'clock in the afternoon, when Pahnke invited them all to tea to recount their experiences, those who had ingested the mushrooms were still so high that all they could do was shake their heads and say wow.

To give some intellectual rigour to what might otherwise have been just a wild Good Friday party, Pahnke had devised a questionnaire in which he singled out nine realms of experience most closely associated with religious mystical experience – things like being in harmony with oneself, the impression that time and space had been transcended, their moods, their feelings of transience, and whether what they had experienced was incapable of being described verbally. The students were asked to complete the questionnaire shortly after the experiment and again six months later.

When the results were analysed, none of the students who had taken the placebo had experienced any of the traits associated with a mystical experience. On the other hand, at least seven of the nine characteristics associated with a mystical experience had been experienced by eight of the ten who had ingested the mushrooms. The conclusions were potentially mind-blowing for the church, dissing the widely held belief that the key to a transcendental religious experience was not asceticism or intense religious devotion but a bag of magic mushrooms. It might just be down to physical brain chemistry.

Alas for Pahnke, although his doctoral thesis was accepted, he lost the funding for his research, Leary was fired, and psychedelic drugs were banned. Pahnke died in a car accident in 1971. Even twenty-five years later, most of the participants described the experiment as one of the high points (literally) of their spiritual lives, and one went so far as to say that it had such a positive effect that it made him want to check out hallucinogens at every available opportunity.

CURIOUS QUESTION
The fourteenth

How flat is a pancake?

There is something curiously appealing about literalism, the state of mind that brooks no deviation from the meaning in front of you. There is no need for curious speculation or theorising. All the hard graft of noodling around a concept has been done for you. In many ways, fundamentalism is an easy street for the brain.

We take so much for granted in our diurnal existence and make comments without hesitating to ponder on whether there is any truth in them. In particular, we pep up our speech with similes. One such is 'X is as flat as a pancake', used rarely in a positive context, it seems to me – but we hardly ever take the time to examine whether the comparators are apt. Just how flat is a pancake? Thank heavens, though, there are members of the scientific community who have the time to help us on our way.

This is where some research conducted by Messrs Fonstad, Pugatch, and Vogt of the Geography Departments of Texas State and Arizona State Universities comes in handy. Our brave researchers sought to demonstrate whether the Midwestern state of Kansas is really as flat as a pancake, as is popularly suggested.

The starting point of the experiment was to buy a well-cooked pancake. From the crepe they took a two-centimetre sample strip that had not had time to dry out. Making use of the digital image processing equipment they had on hand, they took a digitised image of the surface of the pancake from the perspective of a cross section.

Establishing the degree of flatness of Kansas was a bit trickier, but the intrepid team gained access to data from a digital elevation model compiled by the United States Geographical Survey. From that they were able to measure a west-to-east profile across Kansas. Having developed the two comparators, they proceeded to use a geographic information system, another bit of clever software, to calculate the surface transects and produce flatness estimates for both the pancake and for Kansas from data from the digital elevation model.

They assigned a value of 1.0000 to perfect flatness and proceeded to compare the pancake and Kansas against this paradigm of flatness. They found that the flatness value for the pancake was 0.957 – pretty flat, but not the epitome of flatness – whereas the corresponding value for Kansas was 0.997. So Kansas was actually flatter than a pancake.

It would be helpful if this research was extended to other jurisdictions so that, if we take 0.957 as the value for the flatness of a pancake, we can establish which territory has an equivalent value. Then we could develop a simile that would satisfy the literalists, the scientists, and the curious alike.

On a vaguely related topic, philosophers and idlers have wondered which came first, the chicken or the egg. The only way to settle this thorny problem is to conduct an experiment. This is exactly what Alice Shirrell Kaswell did, taking a chicken and an egg, appropriately wrapped and documented, to her local post office in Cambridge, Massachusetts. At 9.40 a.m. on the Monday, both packages were accepted by the obliging mail service and were sent on their merry way to a post office adjacent to Penn Station in the Big Apple.

Neither consignment arrived until the Wednesday, but the chicken arrived in the morning, at 10.31, whereas the egg didn't appear until the evening at 21.37. So there we have it: Empirically, the chicken came before the egg.

Isn't science wonderful?

Can we compare metaphors and similes denoting speed?

The English language is full of metaphors and similes denoting speed. At the drop of a hat, I bet before you know it you can come up with a dozen or so. Most of us are not choosy which one we use at any particular moment. We generally pick either the first that comes to us or that which seems the most apposite. But is there a hierarchy amongst the sayings, and is the one we use really that apposite for the situation we are describing?

Fortunately, some researchers have done the legwork for us. In this particular instance, researchers from the University Campus of Suffolk may take a bow for tabulating in order of speed some twenty of the most commonly used descriptions of velocity.

Not surprisingly, at the top of the list is *at the speed of light*, which travels at three hundred million metres per second. *Lightning fast* comes in at a laggardly six million metres a second. Halley's comet was measured as travelling at 84,909 metres per second when it was observed in May 1910, and this might reasonably be taken as the standard for *like a comet*.

The fastest recorded space shuttle was clocked as travelling at a rate of 8,947 metres a second, and this is good enough to put the description *supersonic* into fourth place. *A speeding bullet* leaves the barrel of a rifle at a speed of 1,524 metres per second, a velocity sufficient to secure it fifth place.

To test the actual velocity of some phrases, the researchers had to carry out some experimentation. To test the speed and therefore the relative ranking of *a drop of a hat*, they dropped the headwear from head height in a vacuum where it wouldn't encounter any air resistance. The recorded speed of 5.7 metres a second put the phrase in a lowly sixteenth place, but this was considerably faster than *a blink of an eye*, the speed of which is 0.003 metres a second, the slowest of the twenty phrases tested.

A peregrine falcon in full swoop (and the origin of the phrase *in one fell swoop*) travels at 108.05 metres a second, the fastest speed of any self-propelled animal but only sufficient to earn it seventh place. If you feel you need to compare speed with a member of the animal kingdom, bear this in mind because a *bat out of hell* weighs in at a lowly 35.8 metres per second, the speed of a Mexican free-tailed bat. Assorted animals that figuratively shoot up things – like a *ferret up a trouser leg* (6.94 metres per second) and a *rat up a drainpipe* (0.893 metres per second) - are considerably tardier.

Make it snappy, the favourite phrase of the impatient, comes in at number thirteen, as the rate at which a finger can be snapped or clicked is around thirteen metres per second, but still faster than *like wildfire* which, mercifully, only spreads at a rate of seven metres per second. *Flick of a switch*, which sounds as though it ought to be quick because it is something mechanical, is down at eighteenth place. A switch fitted with a reed relay and operated automatically by magnet is the fastest way a switch can be flicked, and its speed is just two metres per second.

So there, *before you know it* – eighth place, as electrical impulses travel along the nerves in our body at a rate of one hundred metres a second – you have an interesting table showing the relativity of many of our familiar sayings to describe speed.

Isn't science wonderful?

What is the effect of crystal meth on the memory?

It has been a long time a-coming, but it has finally dawned on me that I am totally unsuited for the wacky world of academia. Take crystal meth, the drug of choice, it seems, of non-executive chairmen of British financial institutions and Canadian mayors. Proponents of the drug claim that it enhances self-esteem and sexual pleasure. On the other hand, it is highly addictive and is a habit that is difficult to break.

What seems to make it a particularly difficult drug to get off is that as an amphetamine-based narcotic, it enhances memory. The pleasurable sensations users experience become deeply ingrained in those recollections they associate with the drug. The impact of crystal meth on the memory is, naturally, an area for psychological research. OK, I'm with this so far.

But the logical quantum leap needed to carry out this line of research is quite beyond my poor grey cells to contemplate, as this report of some research into the matter reported in the *Journal of Experimental Biology* in May 2010 (which came to my attention at a snail's pace) amply illustrates.

Barbara Sorg of the Washington State University started pondering this problem and decided, as only a true denizen of the groves of academe would do, that the correct way to further human understanding was to study the effect of crystal meth on the memory of Lymnaea stagnalis, the humble pond snail.

A stroke of genius, I would say. It would never have crossed my mind to make this connection. After all, ignoramus that I am, I had never associated snails with much of a memory nor, it has to be said, with the ability to communicate their thoughts and sensations.

It seems that this poor mollusc has a very simple neuron network compared with humans but holds memories about when to breathe through their breathing tubes. They breathe through their skin when oxygen levels are high but extend their breathing tubes above the water's surface when oxygen supplies are low. Dropping the snails into de-oxygenated, meth-laced water, the researchers found a dosage (at 1 and 3.3·μmol·l-1 meth, if you want to try it at home) that induced the molluscs to stop raising their breathing tubes.

Having altered their short-term behaviour, what about the impact on the snails' long-term behaviour? The researchers trained the snails to remember to keep their breathing tubes closed when oxygen levels were low by poking them with a stick every time they tried to open them. They subjected the poor molluscs to this training twice an hour for a period of twenty-four hours, the period that snails can hold a memory for.

Twenty-four hours later, when the scientists dropped the molluscs into de-oxygenated water, they found that they had forgotten their training and tried to open their breathing tubes. But when the meth was introduced back into the water, the snails' behaviour changed.

The researchers then decided to test whether exposure to crystal meth actually improved the snails' memories. It did! Exposure to meth allowed them to remember training that normally they would have forgotten. More intriguingly, memories associated with meth seemed more powerful than other memories.

A brief resume like this cannot do justice to the sheer brilliance of this research. The takeaway for ordinary Joes like me is that memories formed as a result of exposure to amphetamines such as crystal meth are strong, recur in environments which the user associates with taking the drug, and can improve memory. The world is a better place for knowing this.

On a practical level, and for the peace of mind of our garden molluscs, I won't hide my stash in the garden pond!

Is the shuffle feature really random?

I have an extensive music collection that I carry around with me on a handy three-inch by two-inch box of tricks in MP3 format. Even twenty years ago it would have seemed inconceivable that I could carry around my complete record collection and access any track at the click of a switch, but I can. And perhaps life is even better for it. What I find I use increasingly more often, because choice requires thought and concentration, which in turn distracts me from doing what I otherwise would be doing, is the shuffle feature on the player. Start off with one track, hit the shuffle button, and let the machine's algorithm select which tracks to play for your listening pleasure. What could be easier?

What I find, though, is that the same tracks appear from time to time whilst other tracks may as well not be in the machine as they never see the light of day. This set me wondering how truly random the shuffle feature really is – a twenty-first-century concern if there ever was one.

Of course, behind this rather diurnal concern is a bigger question: What do we understand by randomness? If we are expecting every track on our MP3 player to be played just once but in an unanticipated order, then this is not random. For there to be true randomness at play, it is likely that the same track or tracks will pop up within the sequence, albeit distributed randomly. The problem is that what is really random may not seem to be random to us.

What we are exposed to, according to those who know about these things, is a phenomenon known as *gambler's fallacy*, also called the *Monte Carlo fallacy*. Simply put, this is the belief (mistaken as it is) that if something happens more often than normal during a period, then it is less likely to happen in the future, and if something hasn't happened in a particular period it is more likely to happen later on. If true randomness is at play, then this cannot be the case because the event is just as likely to happen in the future or not as it did or did not in the past. One consequence of this fallacy is that if we hear a couple of tracks by the same artist in short order, we think there is a problem with the random generator.

Although this makes the phenomenon of the recurring shuffle items more comprehensible, it is not quite as simple as that (surprise, surprise!) because we are at the mercy of inherent deficiencies of the algorithm deployed to generate random numbers. Computers are programmed to be consistent and to deliver the same (correct) answer. In other words they are deterministic, a characteristic that is diametrically opposed to randomness.

Often, in order to give the sense of randomness, programmers will use an algorithm using a pseudo random number generator that starts with a common seed number and follows a pattern. The results are often sufficiently complex to make the pattern difficult to discern, but because the algorithm is carefully defined and consistently repeated, it cannot be truly random.

And then, of course, we compound the problem by turning our MP3 player off because we have lives to lead and we can't spend all our time listening to our music, pleasurable as it may be. Once the player has been turned off and on, many a shuffle feature will start again, which means, depending upon how large or small your collection of tracks is from which it selects, you run the risk of hearing some of the tracks previously selected again.

CURIOUS QUESTION
The eighteenth

Is an empty beer bottle more likely to crack your skull than a full one?

During my travels around our green and pleasant land, I like to seek out pubs that sell unusual beers. Some of the establishments I visit can be a little on the insalubrious side, but fortunately, to date I have not experienced any physical violence.

Of course imbibing alcohol to excess can result in a greater propensity for arguments, and occasionally these exchanges of opinion can end up in violent confrontations. And with beer bottles and glasses in attendance, there are ready weapons at hand. This threat moves us to ask whether a full or empty beer bottle is more likely to crack your skull.

Fortunately, according to a paper published in the *Journal of Forensic and Legal Medicine*, some Swiss researchers have devoted a part of their lives to establishing the answer. The scientists, led by the inestimable Dr Bolliger, selected a half-litre bottle of Feldschosschen to conduct their experiments with.

They used ten bottles, four full and six empty, which they laid on their sides. They dropped a one-kilogram steel ball onto them from varying heights of between two and four metres. They discovered that full beer bottles tolerated energies of up to twenty-five joules but shattered at thirty joules or above. In contrast, an empty bottle needed energies of up to forty joules before they shattered.

So far so good. Experiments conducted to demonstrate the tolerance of human skulls to blows showed that they shattered, depending upon the area struck, by blows with energy values of between 14.1 joules and 68 joules. In other words, if your napper is struck by a beer bottle that shatters, it makes no difference whether it is full or empty at the time of impact. Either will have enough force to potentially fracture your skull. A beer glass, though, shatters at 1.7 joules and is, therefore, unlikely to break your skull.

Worth knowing, I think.

When is the best time to drink a cup of coffee?

I must confess that a cup of strong coffee first thing in the morning sets me up for the day. When I was commuting to London, I purchased my coffee at the wittily named Moo-la-la on Farnborough station, dispensed by Karen with her customary brio and bonhomie. A test of its quality and temperature was that it should last until just before my train reaches Surbiton. Such yardsticks measure our daily existence.

According to a scientific study into the effects of our daily dose of caffeine on our body, the optimal time to ingest the stimulant is between 9.30 a.m. and 11.30 a.m. This is all down to the way that caffeine interacts with a hormone in our body called cortisol, which helps to regulate the body's internal clock and promote alertness. Cortisol is known as the stress hormone because it is secreted in higher levels when the body is responding to stressful situations. It can prompt quick bursts of energy, heighten memory, and lower sensitivity to pain – all valuable for the trials and tribulations of the daily commute.

The scientists report that the cortisol levels in our body are at a natural high shortly after we lift ourselves from our slumbers. They remain at that level for around an hour. If you drink a cup of coffee when the cortisol levels in your blood are high, it has less of an effect. Our innards develop a tolerance for caffeine, and we generally need to take an extra shot to get the desired effect. Far better, they suggest, that we should take our caffeine when the cortisol levels are on the wane.

Cortisol levels in the blood also peak at between noon and 1 p.m. and between 5.30 p.m. and 6.30 p.m., so you may want to factor this into your decision as to when to have your next shot of caffeine. Other researchers have found that drinking coffee in the afternoon can help to offset lapses in attention that occur after a large lunch. Useful knowledge for those city wallahs amongst you!

Of course, the timing of your first cup of coffee, if the research is to be believed, is highly dependent upon what time you get up. I used to rise just before 5.30 a.m., so my 6.15 a.m. coffee was a tad early, but as cortisol levels were beginning to wane, the stimulation that the caffeine brought was not entirely wasted. However, you should think twice about having a shot of coffee as soon as you wake after surfacing from a night on the tiles.

Whatever did we do without these insights into the way our body functions?

Does it take longer to swim through treacle than water?

We use the phrase 'like moving through treacle' as a simile for doing something slowly and with difficulty. For the enquiring mind, the obvious question is – is that really true?

It is a question that has occupied much greater minds than mine. In the seventeenth century, Isaac Newton and Christiaan Huygens considered the question, with Newton arguing that an object's speed would be affected by the viscosity of the fluid through which it was travelling. Huygens took the contrary view – that it would not make a jot of difference. Newton was sufficiently troubled by his colleague's assertion that he included both theories in his *Principia Mathematica*. Not very helpful!

In 2004, Edward Cussler of the University of Minnesota published a paper in the ever popular *American Institute of Chemical Engineers Journal* in which he described the results of his researches into whether humans swim more slowly in syrup than in water. He was ably assisted in his research by a student competitive swimmer, Brian Gettelfinger. Their syrup of choice was guar gum or guaran, which comes from the guar bean, native to India. It is used commercially in the food industry primarily because it binds water, and it takes only small amounts to thicken. Guar is often used in ice cream to improve texture and in gluten-free baking to replace some of the structure lost by removing the glutens.

When you consider it, there are a host of problems to be overcome if you adopt the empirical approach to the conundrum. You need to find sympathetic owners of a swimming pool who will allow you to fill it with syrup. You need enough of the stuff to fill the pool. Then you need to work out how to dispose of it after the experiment is over. Showing the tenacity of a man determined to unravel the truth, Cussler secured the twenty-two separate permissions he needed to conduct the experiment and managed to convince the local authority that it was perfectly safe to empty the syrup down the drains.

So the stage was set for the experiment. Two twenty-five-metre swimming pools were used, one with ordinary water, and the other mixed with more than 300 kilograms of guar syrup, producing a gloopy liquid twice the thickness of water. Sixteen volunteers took part, some competitive and others recreational swimmers, deploying the same strokes in each of the pools. What the researchers found was that irrespective of the strokes used, the swimmers' times differed by no more than 4 per cent. What is more, neither water nor syrup produced consistently faster times. So Huygens was right.

It seems that when you are in syrup, you experience more friction from your movement — what is known as viscous drag — and you generate more forward force from each stroke. In other words, the two cancel each other out. For humans, what determines the speed at which you swim at is not the liquid you are swimming in but the shape you adopt. Once the effects of thrust and friction have cancelled themselves out, the predominant force is form drag, the frontal area presented by the body. The perfect swimmer has powerful muscles but a narrow frontal profile.

However, below a certain threshold of speed and size, viscous drag becomes the dominant force, and in those circumstances, swimming through syrup would be more difficult than through water. Just ask some bacteria.

So now we know!

Why do the British drive on the left?

Here in Britain we like to think we are a cut above the rest, and we revel in those differences that mark out the way we do things from those of our continental brethren. Take driving. Why do we in Britain drive on the left when so many other countries favour the right?

In the good old days, there were only two ways of getting around: by Shank's pony or on horseback. If you were a knight and were on horseback (and right-handed) you would want to ensure that your sword hand was unencumbered to enable you to defend yourself against attackers. Dismounting was also easier on the left, particularly if you had a sword in the way. This meant that horse riders naturally preferred to ride on the left hand side of the pathway, a practice that had been enshrined in legislation by 1300 by Pope Boniface VIII.

Things became a bit more complicated around the eighteenth century when wagons drawn by teams of horses were used to convey heavy loads. The driver didn't have a seat but rode the left rear horse, leaving his right arm free to wield the whip. Because he was sitting on the left, the driver was happier if everyone passed him on the left. In other words, they adopted a preference for driving on the right-hand side.

What gave a real impetus to the driving on the right movement was the French Revolution and subsequent events. The French aristocracy had traditionally ridden on the left, forcing the peasants to travel on the right. When the sans-culottes gained the ascendancy in 1789, they made driving on the right de rigueur. Napoleon's rampages across Europe introduced the trend of driving on the right to many of our European friends.

Naturally, in Britain we eschewed everything that smacked of foreign ways and steadfastly stuck to our guns, ploughing our furrows on the left. The practice was enshrined in legislation here in 1835, and just as Boney had done, we introduced the custom of driving on the left to those parts of the world that had the good fortune to come under the yoke of enlightenment, otherwise known as the British Empire. That is why some 35 per cent of the world's population, including countries such as India, Australia, New Zealand, and some African countries drive on the left to this day. Showing the laissez-faire for which we are famed, some countries such as Egypt, which moved from French to British control, were allowed to retain their French customs.

The Japanese, who were never British subjects, still drive on the left. This is due to their Samurai heritage. They too needed to have their sword hand free. But it wasn't until 1872 that this unwritten custom became official, a year that coincided with the Brits helping the Japanese build their railways. It became enshrined in law in 1924.

The Americans, of course, drive on the right. Initially, when it was a British colony, the inhabitants drove on the left, but following their rebellion in 1776, they forswore all practices they associated with their colonial masters. Of course, the influx of settlers from European countries who had been subjected to the dread influence of the French also helped. The state of Pennsylvania was the first to pass legislation that required people to drive on the right (in 1792), followed by New York (1804), and New Jersey (1813).

The answer, then, is due to knights, Napoleon, and British perversity. So now we know!

How do you make the perfect cream scone?

I must confess I am partial to a Devon cream tea, the highlight of which, of course, is the cream scone. But there are so many dilemmas associated with this treat. How do you pronounce scone? Is it scone, as in *own*, or scone, as in *on*? My preference is for scone as in *own*. How much cream and how much jam should you put on the scone? Should you use only clotted cream? Should you put the jam on first and then the cream or the other way round? How do you keep them from crumbling into pieces when you take the first mouthful?

Relax, dear reader, because help is at hand thanks to some research carried out by Dr Eugenia Cheng, a mathematician at the University of Sheffield. Her research broke the cream tea down into three key elements; scones, cream, and jam. The key to a perfect scone is to follow the weight ratio of 2:1:1 – in other words, a 70 gram scone needs 35 grams of jam and 35 grams of cream. Cheng's research, unsurprisingly, as it was sponsored by Rodda's Cornish Clotted Cream, concludes that clotted cream is better than whipped cream. This is because more whipped cream is required to cover the same area than clotted cream.

The ideal thickness of the scone should be 2.8 centimetres to allow it to fit into the mouth easily, and the jam should be put on first before the cream. Putting the cream on first causes the jam to run off the scone, causing an unholy mess.

The key to successful construction of the perfect scone is to ensure that the cream is the same thickness as the scone, otherwise the cream will topple off, and you need to ensure that there is a rim of five millimetres between the scone and the jam and a further rim of five millimetres between the jam and the cream. Compliance with these instructions will ensure that you have the perfect scone, which will neither collapse nor drip.

Frustratingly, Cheng does not address the question of how the word *scone* should be pronounced.

The pursuit of perfection is all well and good, but some naysayers opine that one of the joys of eating a cream scone is the mess you get into. I suppose it is, as is often the case, a question of paying your money and taking your choice.

But at least we now know!

The twenty-third

Why does mown grass smell so fresh?

In our household TOWT is the gardener. I am confined to maintenance duties aka mowing the lawn, the size of which reduces annually as she takes up more of the garden with her borders. My dream of having a sit-on mower is rapidly fading into the distance.

Still, one of the undeniable benefits of being consigned to manicuring the lawn is the marvellous aroma of freshly mown grass. That and the smells of a garden immediately after a shower are, to my mind, two of the most wonderful and quintessential smells of an English summer. But what causes the newly mown grass to smell so fresh?

It's the grass releasing organic compounds called *green leaf volatiles* (GLVs), which are part of the plant's defence mechanism. The release of GLVs has a number of purposes. First, in response to the trauma of having its head chopped off, the grass uses the GLVs to stimulate the formation of new cells around the blade's wound to repair the damage. Some of the GLVs act as a kind of antibiotic to prevent bacterial infection and to minimise fungal growth. Some GLVs combine with other chemicals in the plant to produce what might be termed a distress signal to warn other parts of your lawn of the fate that is about to befall them. Interestingly, some plants use GLVs as a means of making insects that are munching them more attractive to their predators.

It is not just humans who prompt this release of GLVs. All leafy plants seem to generate GLVs to a greater or lesser extent, and so any creature, be it a herbivore or an insect, or any implement deployed by Homo sapiens may cause it to happen. The specific and distinctive whiff released by traumatised grass is due to eight related and oxygenated hydrocarbons, the heady cocktail of which includes aldehydes and alcohols. I suppose we are not so aware of the odour when cattle or sheep are grazing on grass because they do not cause so much damage to such a large expanse of grass in so short a time. That and in my experience, they are busily creating other odours that overpower the smell of the grass.

As is always the way these days, we can't just luxuriate in this wonderful aroma without some spoilsport wanting to pour a bucket of cold water over our enjoyment. According to some Aussie researchers, the compounds that contribute to the aroma are precursors to ozone formation and may assist in the creation of smog in cities and towns. You know what? I don't care if they do. Sometimes you just have to appreciate the simple pleasures of life.

I'm off to get my fix – the lawn beckons!

CURIOUS QUESTION
The twenty-fourth

Can you compare an apple with an orange?

I have been in enough meetings during my career where one or more of the participants have been accused of comparing apples with oranges, the inference being that two concepts are so dissimilar that they are incapable of being compared with each other. It is now an accepted idiom in everyday speech. But is it an appropriate analogy?

Thank heavens there is someone in the scientific community who has taken up the challenge. Step forward Scott A Sandford of the NASA Ames Research Centre in California (natch). He took an apple (Granny Smith, I believe) and a Sunkist Orange and prepared the samples by desiccating them in a convection oven at a low temperature over a number of days. After mixing the dried samples with potassium bromide and grinding them for a couple of minutes in a small ball-bearinged mill, Sandford pressed the resultant powders into a circular pellet and then subjected them to spectroscopic analysis.

The results of the analysis were that apples and oranges are indeed similar and that it was (relatively) easy to compare them. I'm not sure I would agree that Sandford's elaborate preparation of the samples was easy. If I have a few spare days and a spare spectroscope, I might give it a go. But the key finding is that there is no basis for the analogy. The next time anyone accuses you of comparing apples with oranges, you can say 'Precisely, you have made my point'.

Of course, those of us who delight in the etymology of words and phrases will smile smugly in the knowledge that the phrase was originally somewhat different, as this exchange between Tranio and Biondello in Shakespeare's *Taming of the Shrew* shows:

> T: He is my father, sir; and, sooth to say,
>   In countenance somewhat doth resemble you.

> B: [aside] As much as an apple doth an oyster, and all one.

I would like to see Sandford deconstruct that analogy!

I don't know much about cats, but popular conceptions about them are that they have nine lives and always land on their feet, even when dropped upside down. I was pleased to discover that an intrepid member of the research community, braving the wrath and opprobrium of the animal welfare brigade, has set about to prove my second statement in a systematic way. Fiorella Gambale from Milan took a cat, turned it upside down, and dropped it from various heights – one hundred times each from heights between six feet and one foot, descending by intervals of a foot a time.

The results were that in every case, over five hundred instances, the cat landed upright on its feet when dropped from heights of between six feet and two feet. However, when the moggy was dropped from a height of one foot, it never once landed on its feet.

No explanation for this baffling phenomenon is proffered by la Gambale, but I suspect that the distance travelled and the speed at which the cat drops are insufficient to allow it to perform the necessary acrobatics to right itself. Perhaps inadvertently, in carrying out the experiment, she also confirmed that a cat has (at least) nine lives!

Has man come to the end of the evolutionary road?

Charles Darwin – or was it Alfred Russel Wallace? – really put the cat amongst the finches when he came up with his theory of evolution. Until that point it was kind of comforting and easily intelligible to accept that man was the acme of a grand master plan controlled by an omnipotent deity. Homo sapiens was as good as life was going to get, the top of the tree of life.

The underlying concept of evolution is that life, in all its forms, is constantly adapting, or at least trying to adapt, to its environment. Those that succeed thrive, and those that don't fall by the wayside. This is the classic cause of evolution: The struggle of the fittest to survive.

But there are other causes that prompt the evolutionary process. There is genetic drift where chance factors cause random changes in the frequency of traits. There is mutation caused by changes in the composition of DNA. There is gene flow where changes occur because the life form moves from one place to another and has offspring in the new place. And there is non-random mating where the life form actively selects individuals with particular traits with whom to mate.

For the enquiring mind that accepts the basic concept of evolution, the big question is whether Homo sapiens is still evolving. Perhaps it is because we consider ourselves to be the platonic paradigm of evolution that it is a little difficult to accept that there are still changes happening to our genetic make-up. Are we just a link in an evolutionary progression? If we adopt a longer-term view, a number of factors suggest that we are still evolving.

The first relates to the ability to drink milk. Originally, the gene that enabled us to digest lactose shut down when, as babies, we were weaned off our mother's breast milk. The move away from hunter-gatherer societies to ones that cultivated crops and domesticated animals meant that there was a plentiful supply of milk. Ability to digest lactose became a nutritionally advantageous quality, and individuals who were able to digest lactose were better able to pass on their genes. Of Northern Europeans, 95 per cent now carry the genetic mutation enabling them to digest lactose.

Wisdom teeth have always seemed to me to be an unnecessary encumbrance. They are a vestige of a period of man's development when they developed a third set of choppers. Their jaws were bigger, and their diet meant that they wore out their teeth more quickly than we do. Today around 35 per cent of the population are born without the ability to develop wisdom teeth.

Our environment is full of germs that are potentially inimical to our general well-being. Over time we have developed genes that are geared mainly to fight disease. Researchers reckon some 1,800 genes have been developed in humans over the last forty thousand years for this very purpose. More than a dozen genetic variations designed to resist malaria are spreading rapidly amongst those living in the continent of Africa.

Our brains are reducing in size, with capacity shrinking over the last 30,000 years from 1,500 cubic centimetres to 1,350. This is not because we are getting stupider. It is because the processing capabilities of our little grey cells are becoming more efficient.

Consider also blue eyes. Until around ten thousand years ago, all Homo sapiens had brown eyes. Then some genetic mutation occurred which turned brown eyes into blue.

So if we take a long-term view of our species, we are still plodding along the evolutionary journey. I wonder where we will end up?

Why is a day divided into twenty-four hours?

We are all slaves to time to some degree. It regulates our daily life, and, if you are not careful, it can take over completely. It is a puzzling concept, not least because the way we notate the passage of time is rooted in a base twelve numeric system that to those of us who are used to the base ten system seems a tad archaic. With a bit of it on my hands, I started to wonder why this was so.

The culprits, if you choose to think of them in that way, are the Sumerians by way of the ancient Egyptians. Although it is clear from hieroglyphs dating back to as early as 3000 BCE that Egyptians were using a base ten decimal counting system, they inherited and adopted a base twelve system from the Sumerians. Why twelve? It was based on the three knuckles in each of the four fingers of your hand.

When they considered the concept of time, the Egyptians looked to the heavens. In particular, they tracked a series of thirty-six small constellations, known as *decans*, which rise consecutively over the horizon at approximately forty-minute intervals. The rising of each decan marked the start of a new hour. A *decade* – a ten-day period – began with the appearance of a new decan in the eastern sky just before dawn.

By 2100 BCE, the Egyptians had created a unified annual calendar consisting of thirty-six decades, constituting a 360-day year. This system proved accurate enough to predict the annual flooding of the Nile, so critical for their agricultural system.

During the New Kingdom (approximately 1550 to 1070 BCE), the measuring system was simplified to use a set of twenty-four stars, twelve marking daytime and twelve night-time. Once the light and dark hours had been divided into twelve parts, the concept of a twenty-four-hour day was in place. However, the length of each hour varied according to the seasons, and it was not until the Hellenistic period and in particular Hipparchus (active between 147 and 127 BCE) that the concept of a fixed-time period was developed.

Hipparchus proposed dividing the day into twenty-four equinoctial hours, based on the twelve hours of daylight and twelve hours of darkness observed on equinox days. Despite this suggestion, laypeople continued to use seasonally varying hours for many centuries. Hours of fixed length became commonplace only after mechanical clocks first appeared in Europe during the fourteenth century.

Hipparchus and other Greek astronomers adopted astronomical techniques developed by the Babylonians, who operated a sexagesimal (base sixty) counting system. Guess who they got it from? Right in one, the Sumerians. Why they used a sexagesimal counting system is unclear, although it is convenient for expressing fractions. After all, it is the smallest number equally divisible by each of the first six numbers, as well as by ten, twelve, fifteen, twenty, and thirty.

Those who had a penchant for a decimal-based system made a couple of attempts to establish it. The French in 1793, imbued with revolutionary fervour, introduced French Revolutionary Time: a ten-hour day, with one hundred minutes an hour and one hundred seconds per minute. It was introduced officially on 24 November 1793 but was deeply unpopular and abandoned on 7 April 1795.

The French had another go in 1897. The Bureau des longitudes established the Commission de décimalisation du temps under the direction of a mathematician, Henri Poincare, to devise a decimal system. As is the way with committees, it was a bit of a compromise, retaining the twenty-four-hour day but dividing the hour into one hundred minutes and the minutes into one hundred seconds. It didn't gain much support, and the idea was quietly dropped in 1900.

Decimalisation has started creeping in by the back door. Clocks that track workers' starting and finishing times use decimals to record parts of hours. And of course it is easier to denote a part of an hour with decimal notation if you are using a word processing package. But it seems as though we are stuck with our antiquated system of denoting time. Blame the Sumerians, I say.

How long is a generation?

We talk glibly of once in a generation or the baby boomer generation, but it dawned on me the other day that I really don't have a clue how long a generation is or how a generation is defined. Since the purpose of this book is to shed light on those nagging questions or doubts that creep into the subconscious, I decided to find out. Unsurprisingly, the answer isn't quite as straightforward as you might expect or hope for.

Some people are deeply fascinated with genealogy. Many of us are keen to explore our family history in hope of finding the key to a lost fortune or to expose a skeleton that will give us kudos at the next dinner party. Generally we are disappointed, or our research peters out down some dead end. But the key to genealogy is developing a family tree that shows X begat Y.

The firstborn of parents A and B could legitimately (or in some cases illegitimately) be called the start of the next generation. Indeed, this is what is known as a biological generation. The problem is that its duration is specific to each couple and does not have a fixed length. So it is handy for the specific: I am the fourth generation from Joe Bloggs. However, it is not really that helpful as a generality and even within one branch of a family will be a bit of a moveable feast.

By consolidating a whole host of biological generations, we can develop a familial generation, a sort of rule of thumb that says (broadly) that the age at which a woman bears her firstborn is Y. Aeons ago, the value associated with a familial generation was as low as twenty years – the result of a combination of lower overall life expectancy, earlier marriages, and larger families – but these days it is more likely to be around the twenty-five-year mark or, recognising the trend in certain societies for women to have their firstborn nowadays even later, as high as twenty-eight. This in itself brings a whole lot of problems with it because it is a sliding scale. Twenty-eight may be appropriate today but would be over-egging it by some if we were talking about life a century or so ago.

The next concept is that of a societal generation. This owes its genesis to the French lexicographer Emile Littre, who in 1863 defined a generation as 'all men living more or less at the same time'. The key characteristics are that a bunch of people are born around the same period of time and have exposure to the same formative historical and cultural experiences. So we talk of the 'lost generation': those who were born in time to live through or perish during the First World War – or the 'baby boomers': those who never had it so good and were born between the end of the Second World War and the early 1960s. It is a useful form of shorthand to define an era or a set of shared beliefs or experiences, but for those looking for numerical exactitude, it is all a bit wishy-washy.

The other end of the spectrum is what is termed 'designated generations', where the age for reaching a particular stage in your life cycle is firmly prescribed and static. An example would be the culture of the East African Pokots. All the key things a male can or cannot do are defined by their age, whether it be marriage or the type of hairstyle. Whilst this approach doesn't take into account biological changes such as increased life expectancy, there is a pleasing degree of certainty with it.

So frustratingly, there is no real answer to what should have been a fairly straightforward question.

The twenty-eighth

When are you grown up?

'Grow up' and 'act your age' are popular refrains of exasperated parents, but these phrases, rather like our glib use of *generation*, require us to answer the question, When are we grown up? Of course, there is a fairly simple biological answer. The body reaches physical maturity between the ages of 18 and 21 by virtue of the fact that we stop growing, upwards if not outwards. And those ages tend to mark out, in legislation, the formal line that separates childhood from adulthood.

What were simple demarcations are now being muddied, first by a trend by legislators to push more responsibility on to those who are even younger (I am thinking primarily of the bandwagon to give the vote to 16-year-olds) and second, by a greater dependence of our offspring on their parents, at least for accommodation and financial assistance, well into their twenties and beyond. If what marks out a child from an adult is dependency for the basics, then childhood is extending rather than contracting. Perhaps, rather than the purely biological and legal distinction, there are social and psychological factors that determine when we have grown up.

In an attempt to resolve this line of enquiry, I looked up a survey that asked two thousand people over the age of 18 what were the factors that made them believe they had reached adulthood.

The triggers for feeling that they had become an adult are interesting, quite sad, and portray a rather strange view of the more mature set. Of those who answered, 68 per cent said that the key rite of passage was buying their first home; 63 per cent thought the patter of tiny feet; and 52 per cent said getting married were decisive moments.

More boring activities such as paying into a pension (29 per cent), becoming house-proud (22 per cent), and taking out life insurance (21 per cent) were signs of adulthood to some. Quaintly, some thought that looking forward to a night at home (21 per cent), doing DIY projects (18 per cent), hosting dinner parties (18 per cent), and having a joint bank account (17 per cent) were features that marked the transition to being an adult.

To these respondents unearthed by Beagle Street, the main characteristic that meant that you had *not* reached psychological adulthood was a reliance on your parents (42 per cent). Other symptoms were living at home (36 per cent), playing computer games (31 per cent), watching children's movies (30 per cent), and watching cartoons (29 per cent). Perhaps more alarmingly, key reasons why the respondents didn't feel like adults included a fear of growing up and taking responsibility (28 per cent), not wanting a "real" or nine-to-five job (22 per cent), a desire to travel and see the world, and idolising juvenile role models (20 per cent each).

On average, the respondents felt that they reached or were likely to reach adulthood at the grand old age of 29.

So there we have it, straight from the mouths of babes. And with the price of housing becoming ever more unaffordable and the scandalous dearth of good quality, affordable rented accommodation coupled with the high levels of youth unemployment, this trend towards adult infantilism is likely to remain with us, meaning the boundary between childhood and adulthood will extend ever outwards. A grim prospect indeed.

And it provokes a couple of questions too big for this book to consider: Would a dose of nanny-statism reduce the divide between the start of chronological and psychological adulthood? And should the legislative definition of adulthood move nearer towards the psychological definition? We live in strange times.

Which jumps furthest - a cat flea or a dog flea?

One of my principal objections to having pets, over and above the amount of care and attention they require, is what they carry with them, that is, fleas. If you accept that fleas go with the territory – cats host Ctenocephalides felis whilst dogs harbour Ctenocephalides canis – the natural question that occurs to the enquiring mind is, Which of the two jumps the highest?

It should come as no surprise that a group of scientists have devoted some of their time and research budget to push out the boundaries of human knowledge in this particular case. We are indebted to Messieurs Cadiergues, Joubert, and Franc from the Ecole Nationale Veterinaire de Toulouse for their time and trouble. Their findings were faithfully recorded in 2000 in the ever popular *Veterinary Pathology*.

In order to conduct the experiment, they used a grey plastic cylinder nine centimetres in diameter whose height they were able to raise a centimetre at a time, starting at one and finishing at thirty, as they do in high jump competitions. Groups of ten fleas from the same species were placed at the base of the cylinder, and their jumps were observed and recorded.

The mean jump recorded for the cat fleas was 13.2 centimetres, about 5.2 inches in old money, or over forty times their body length, with the highest jump recorded at 17 centimetres. The dog fleas, on the other hand, outperformed their feline-based rivals, jumping on average 15.5 centimetres and recording a high of 25 centimetres.

When the scientists turned to investigating length of jumps, it was the same story. C felis came in with an average length of jump of 19.9 centimetres with a deviation of plus or minus 9.1. Their longest leap was 48 centimetres, and the lowest a paltry 2 centimetres. C canis, on the other hand, would jump on average 30.4 centimetres, plus or minus 9.1, with the longest leap recorded at 50 centimetres and the shortest at 3 centimetres. So the dog fleas won hands down.

In case you were wondering (and I hope you were), the human flea, pulex irritans, records similar results for height and distance to C felis.

What is the correlation between being bitten by a cat and depression?

Life is full of seemingly random events that individually don't seem to make sense but, when linked with other random events, paint an interesting picture. Take being bitten by a moggy and depression. Thank heavens there are scientists who are prepared to investigate disparate bits of data in the hope of making sense of a bigger picture. Quite why D A Hanauer, N Ramakrishnan and L S Seyfried chose to investigate the linkage between cat bites and depression is anyone's guess, but their findings, published in the *PLOS One* journal, are fascinating nonetheless.

Their starting point was the 1.3 million or so electronic health records held by the University of Michigan Health system, dating back to 1998. They isolated the records of some 117,000 patients over the age of 18, showing one of the twenty-six codes allocated to describe depression. Then they identified the records of all patients over the age of 18 whose records recorded some form of non-venomous animal bites or injuries.

When the researchers correlated the data sets, they came up with some astonishing results. It seems 41.3 per cent of patients who had been bitten by cats had also been diagnosed with depression, and some 28.7 per cent who had been bitten by pooches had also suffered from the blues. Moreover, 85.5 per cent of those patients who had suffered both a cat bite and depression were women compared with 64.5 per cent who had both been bitten by a dog and diagnosed as being medically depressed.

If a woman had sustained a bite from a moggy serious enough to trouble the medics, there was a 47 per cent chance of her being diagnosed with depression at some point in her life. There was a 24.2 per cent chance of a man being diagnosed with depression if he had been bitten by a cat somewhere along the line. Interestingly, the probability of a depression diagnosis reduced to 35.8 per cent in women if they had been bitten by a dog. The corresponding probability for men was 21.1 per cent.

The study also showed that the majority of the bites inflicted on patients were from the patient's own moggy. Being bitten by a stray or feral cat was the least common, although there was a very high incidence of depression amongst women who had been bitten by strays.

What to make of all this? The report draws no firm conclusions, save to make a desperate pitch for more funding with the throw-away comment 'while no causative link is known to explain this association, there is growing evidence to suggest that the relationship between cats and human mental illness, such as depression, warrants further investigation'. Quite.

I suppose there are two ways to look at this. If the moggy that you have lavished lots of love and attention on – not to mention money on those expensive vets' bills and treats – turns round and bites you, you are going to be pretty peed off. For those of a sensitive disposition, this might be just enough to tip you over the edge. On the other hand, cats are predators, and all predators seek out the weakest amongst their prey. It saves them a lot of trouble and effort in the long run. Perhaps the moggy is using some innate hunting instinct to recognise that their owner has some form of vulnerability and pounces. Makes a bit of sense, I suppose.

Perhaps it is best to play safe by giving your cat the order of the boot to preserve your sanity.

What are the signs of a midlife crisis?

I am of an age that encourages me to cling fondly to the conceit that 60 is the new 40. That being the case, I can still look forward to the arrival of a midlife crisis which, according to a new survey, strikes males at the age of 43 and the fairer sex at 44. Typically, the crisis can last between three and ten years for men but only two to five years for women, who are then beset by more pressing biological issues.

The *Telegraph*, the paper of choice for 40-year-olds who think they are 60, has helpfully listed forty signs of the onset of a midlife crisis, a term that was first coined in 1965. The purpose of this book is to unlock some of the mysteries of our existence, and so for your edification and instruction, I reveal a few of the more interesting signs.

Some of the pointers can be characterised as lifestyle choices: the desire for a simpler life or thinking about quitting your job and buying a bed and breakfast business or a pub.

Some can be characterised as an attempt to regain your youth: going to music festivals like Glastonbury or reunion tours of your favourite bands of the seventies and eighties, giving up on Radio 2 and starting to listen to 6 Music, revisiting places you used to holiday at as a child, excessive reminiscing about your childhood, and embracing social media to make you seem cool and on-trend.

The onset of a midlife crisis can cause you to seek a new hobby or to have a sudden desire to play a musical instrument or splash out on an expensive bike.

Vanity also kicks in as you attempt to recreate your youthful vim and vigour: fretting about thinning hair, looking longingly at old photos of yourself, obsessively comparing how you look with the appearance of your contemporaries, starting to dye your hair, stopping telling people your age, contemplating having a hair transplant or plastic surgery, and starting to take vitamin pills.

You are also beset by the grim reality of your predicament: the realisation that you will never pay off your mortgage or that you will never be able to quit your job because you can't afford to or that you will be worse off in retirement than your parents.

Your recuperative powers start to wane. Hangovers get worse and last longer, and your rest is disturbed by worries about work, particularly that someone younger is going to take your job. You find that the only time you read a book is when you are on holiday and that you are easily distracted.

These all make for a fairly depressing litany of symptoms, but many of them resonate with me. I was going to recount them all, but something else caught my attention. Still, at least we now know!

CURIOUS QUESTION
The thirty-second

Why do the best ideas come when you are in the bath?

Have you noticed that your best ideas come when you are doing something that you can do pretty much on autopilot, like washing yourself or exercising or, heaven forfend, working? Why is that, you probably haven't wondered?

It is all down to the fact that these activities don't require much brain power. You can almost literally do them in your sleep. In fact, they relax the prefrontal cortex, which is the control centre for decisions, goals, and behaviour, and switch off your default mode network. These are, so researchers claim, optimal conditions for allowing your brain to develop and explore new and creative connections that, in more stressful conditions, your mind would have dismissed or ignored.

Your brain isn't at its most active when you are focused on a task. Rather it's more active when it's roaming around, looking for something to fix on, making lots of minor computations that come to naught.

And when you are really relaxed – say, soaking in a bath – that state of bliss triggers the release of dopamine, which is a neurotransmitter, a rush of which can stimulate your creative juices. Dopamine also encourages alpha waves to ripple through your brain. They are present when you are meditating or feeling spaced out.

Another magic ingredient to whet your inner creative self is fatigue. A state of tiredness means that your brain is less able to keep away the sort of distracting and seemingly irrelevant thoughts that are the seeds of a great brain wave. You often take a bath when you have just woken up or before you go to bed, when fatigue is at its greatest.

If you want proof that for great ideas you should hop into a bath, look no further than Archimedes. The ancient mathematician was set a challenge by Hiero II. A goldsmith, commissioned to make a votive crown from gold donated by the Syracusan tyrant, was suspected of substituting base metals for some of the gold and Archimedes' task was to establish the truth. This had to be done conclusively and without damaging the crown.

Whilst taking a bath, the Greek sage noticed that the level of the water in the tub rose and that this knowledge could be used to work out the volume of an object. He arrived at the density of the crown by dividing the weight of it by the volume of the water displaced. Cheaper and less dense metals would reduce the density of the crown and, therefore, would displace less water. Inevitably, Archimedes' eureka moment proved that the goldsmith had, indeed, been dishonest.

?

Why do you feel cold when you step out of a shower?

As an Englishman, naturally, I don't take baths. Of course, I find the tub a convenient receptacle in which to store our coal. That said, I do take a daily shower. But why is it, when I step out of a nice warm shower, I suddenly feel cold?

The answer, it seems, is all to do with evaporation, the process by which your body stays cool, normally by sweating. Your body releases moisture that is warmed by your body and disperses it into the general atmosphere. Any movement of air across your body will evaporate moisture. While you are in the shower, the amount of evaporation is minimal because the air within the cubicle is saturated with water vapour. However, as soon as you step out of the shower cubicle into the general bathroom area, the air your body encounters does not have much water vapour. This means that the evaporation process can speed up.

In order to change into a gas, water needs to acquire energy. It does so by sucking up the heat energy in the drops of water that remain on your body. As the water on your body cools, so do you. Your body detects the temperature change and triggers an over-cold reaction. You need to move so that the heat generated by your muscles can warm you up. Otherwise you will get an involuntary muscular spasm, known as *shivering*.

The effect is most noticeable during the winter, when the ambient temperature is lower than that of the shower cubicle you have left. Of course, if you are having a shower in a hot and steamy climate, the effect of having a shower and stepping out of it can feel pleasant.

But if the sensation is too uncomfortable for you, it may be appropriate to consider a Spartan cold shower. The shock of the cold water can startle your groggy body into alertness and can relieve you of fatigue. Cold showers are supposed to be good for those suffering from depression. And because they cause hydration, they can be better for your hair and skin than hot showers. Conversely, hot showers can relieve tensions, soothe stiff muscles, and ease anxiety by increasing your oxytocin levels and moisturising your nasal passages.

For me, I will put up with the minor inconvenience of feeling a bit chilly when I step out of the shower. But at least I now know why!

Why do we wake just before the alarm goes off?

Have you noticed how you invariably become conscious just before the dreaded alarm goes off? It happens to me so often I feel I could dispense with the automated warning that it is time to get up. But without that safety net there, I'm worried whether I would come to at the right time. Why does this happen, I wondered?

It is all down to your circadian rhythm, which in turn is controlled by a group of nerves nestled in the centre of your brain called the *suprachiasmatic nucleus*. In addition to controlling your body clock (when you feel wide awake and sleepy), it also controls your blood pressure, body temperature, and your sense of time. Naturally, your body is most efficient when it follows some form of routine. If you are regular in your habits – go to bed at roughly the same time each day and get up roughly at the same hour – your body locks into that routine.

Your sleep-wake cycle is regulated by a protein called PER, the level of which varies each day, peaking in the evening and plummeting at night. An hour or so before you are supposed to wake, the level of PER rises (along with your body temperature and blood pressure), and in preparation for you coming to, your body releases a cocktail of stress hormones. Your sleep gets lighter and lighter. Following a regular routine means that your body has prepared itself for your rising to coincide almost to the second to the time your alarm goes off.

That being the case, the worst thing you can do is to press the snooze button, turn over, and have another ten minutes, tempting as it might be. Your body is primed to get up, so delaying the process sends it into a deep state of discombobulation as hormones associated with sleeping interfere with the hormones preparing you to get up. The result is you feel groggy and have ensured that you will be starting the day in less than peak condition.

It seems that you can will yourself to wake up at a certain time. It is always a nightmare of mine when I have to get up especially early to catch a plane that I will sleep through. According to research conducted by the University of Lübeck and reported in *Psychology Today*, fifteen volunteers were recruited to sleep in a lab for three nights. On one night they were told they would be woken up at 6 a.m. and on the other nights at 9 a.m. However, the devious researchers woke them up at 6.30 a.m. each day. On days they thought they were getting up early, the sleepers' stress hormones started to increase from 4.30 a.m. On days when they thought they were in for a lie-in, the stress hormones hadn't started to kick in, and so when they were roused, they felt groggy. The conclusion: Our bodies start to prepare us for getting up at the time we think we are getting up.

And finally, if you don't stir before your alarm, you're not getting enough sleep!

So now we know!

What is the best way to deal with a hangover?

I must confess that I am partial to a few drops of the electric sauce. Have you noticed that after having one over the eight and laying down your weary, aching head on the pillow, the room seems to go round and round? Have you ever tried to gather what few grey cells are still functioning to wonder why that is?

It seems that this phenomenon is all down to the effect that alcohol has on your ears and, in particular, on three semicircular canals. These canals contain a fluid called *endolymph* and a gelatinous structure filled with cells covered in fine hair-like stereocilia called *cupula*. Alcohol thins your blood, and when the red stuff gets to the inner ear, it creates a difference in density between the cupula and the endolymph. The little hairs in the cupula bend. In normal circumstances they send a signal to the brain telling you that your position has changed.

Under the influence of alcohol, they are tricked into thinking that you are moving and send signals to the brain that makes it believe that you are rotating – hence the feeling that the room is moving even though you are motionless. If you close your eyes whilst experiencing this phenomenon, it just makes the sensation worse because you have no visual point of reference to contradict the illusion. My best advice for you in these circumstances is to open your eyes and stare at a fixed object.

The next problem, after a few hours of fitful sleep, is that you wake up with an enormous headache, you are good for nothing, and you are on the search for a pick-me-up. The efficacy of your hangover cure is entirely dependent upon how quickly it reduces what acetaldehyde is left in the body. Our livers, or what is left of them, release an enzyme called *alcohol dehydrogenase*, which gets to work on the ethanol content in alcohol to form a chemical called *acetaldehyde*. This in turn is broken down by an enzyme called *aldehyde dehydrogenase* (ALDH) into a chemical called *acetate*. Once this has been accomplished, your feeling of normality and at ease with the world returns.

Perhaps one of the most famous and, by all accounts, efficacious of hangover cures is Jeeves's pick-me-up as described in P G Wodehouse's *Jeeves Takes Charge*:

> 'If you would drink this, sir,' he said, with a kind of bedside manner, rather like the royal doctor shooting the bracer into the sick prince. 'It is a little preparation of my own invention. It is the Worcester sauce that gives it its colour. The raw egg makes it nutritious. The red pepper gives it its bite. Gentlemen have told me they find it extremely invigorating after a late evening.'

Chinese scientists, as reported in *Chemistry World*, have carried out research into the restorative powers of fifty-seven drinks and potions, although not Jeeves's panacea. The most efficacious of the drinks for reducing the effects of alcohol on the body and promoting the ADLH process proved to be Sprite, that colourless, lemon and lime, caffeine-free soft fizzy drink that was developed by the Coca-Cola company in the early 1960s to counter the popularity of 7 Up. Some trendier and allegedly healthier hangover cures such as herbal tea actually make matters worse by inhibiting the ALDH process.

Reluctant as I am to promote the cause of an American multinational, needs must in these circumstances. I am keen to see if it works!

Why do we blush?

Some people seem to be more susceptible to blushing than others. We of a hard-hearted disposition are little troubled by this phenomenon, but we notice it amongst our more sensitive brethren. It is all to do with our sympathetic nervous system and is an involuntary response to a set of stimuli, normally situations in which we feel embarrassed.

Embarrassment causes our body to release adrenaline, our natural hormonal response to fight or flight situations. Our breathing and heart rates increase as if we were preparing to flee the scene, and our pupils dilate so that we absorb as much visual information as possible. Adrenaline can also slow down our digestive processes so that our energy can be directed to our muscles.

Adrenaline has an important effect on our blood vessels, causing them to widen, a process known as *vasodilation*, which has the effect of improving the flow of blood and oxygen around our body. When we blush, the veins in our faces respond to a signal produced by the chemical transmitter *adenylyl cyclase*. They start to dilate, causing more blood than usual to flow into our cheeks. The result? That crimson glow that is symptomatic of the feeling of embarrassment.

What is unusual about blushing is that adrenaline doesn't normally have any effect on our veins. It is only the particular circumstances which give rise to embarrassment that cause this phenomenon.

Scientists do not know for sure why we humans are susceptible to blushing. One theory is that it is a sign of emotional intelligence because to show embarrassment we have to be sympathetic to how others may feel. The tendency to blush seems to develop in young children in step with their growing awareness of others. It is also thought that the ability to blush may be a reflex response that signals regret for what someone has just done and thus avoids any nasty physical consequences for their faux pas. The other person (the theory goes) will find it more difficult to direct an angry response at you if you are blushing like a beetroot.

Some people are embarrassed by their propensity to blush, and some even develop a phobia known as *erythrophobia*. If you are really concerned about turning crimson at the drop of a hat, you can have some surgical correction. A procedure called *endothoracic sympathectomy*, which involves snipping the tiny nerves in your spine that control blushing, seems to do the trick. That seems a bit extreme to me. Far better would be to develop a heart of steel.

How likely are you to be killed by something falling out of space?

As a collector of strange deaths, I got pretty excited in early February 2016 when news filtered through that a man had been killed in mysterious circumstances in the Tamil Nadu district of Vellore in India. Standing by a college café, the poor man, a bus driver, was killed by an explosion, and three bystanders were injured. A black, pockmarked stone was recovered from the five-foot-deep, two-foot-wide crater, and the story soon spread that a meteorite had done it. Had that been the case, it would have been the first death by meteorite to be scientifically proven.

Unfortunately, the scientists have poured cold water over the initial theory of causation. There were no meteorite showers anticipated in the area at the time, and no meteorites were actually observed. NASA went further by saying that the crater looked like one formed by a land-based explosion, and anyway, the fragment of supposed meteorite was nothing more than a bit of common earth rock. So the story fizzled out.

But it left me wondering: How likely is it to be killed by something falling out of space? After all, there are enough rocks and man-made hardware whizzing around. Fortunately, the ever popular *International Comet Quarterly* keeps a scorecard of all the locations and sizes of meteorites that are reported to have landed on earth since the start of the nineteenth century. It is disappointing that its appearance is regular rather than requiring the computational genius of an Edmond Halley to spot it – a marketing trick missed, I feel.

The list is fascinating, and some of the highlights are worth passing on. The first occurrence listed was on 14 December 1807 in Weston, Connecticut, when a meteor was visible for around half a minute. Loud sounds were heard, and many stones weighing in total two hundred pounds, the largest thirty-five pounds, were found scattered in a six- to ten-mile radius. On 16 January 1825 in Oriang in India, a man was reported to have been killed by a meteorite that is said to have also injured a woman. A horse was struck and killed by a meteorite on 1 May 1860 in New Concord, Ohio.

Houses seem to have come off particularly badly. In Hauptmannsdorf in Bohemia in 1847, a thirty-seven-pound Braunau iron meteorite smashed into a room, covering three children with ceiling debris, leaving them shaken but unharmed. In Latvia in 1863, a 5.4-kilogram meteorite penetrated through the roof and embedded itself in the floor, as did a 1-kilogram meteorite in Constantia in South Africa in 1906. In 1954 Mrs Hewlett Hodges was slightly injured when a meteorite crashed through the roof of her house in Sylacauga, Alabama.

Perhaps the most serious occurrence in modern times happened in 1908 in Tunguska in Siberia. The air blast from an object entering the earth's atmosphere is said to have flattened hundreds of square miles of forest, killing two men and hundreds of reindeer. No evidence of a meteorite having landed was ever found. And in February 2013 in Chelyabinsk, meteorites splintered off from a meteor that had hit the earth's atmosphere, injuring some 1,200 people, including two hundred children. The majority of the injuries sustained were from flying glass.

According to a recently published study by the American National Safety Council, the odds of being killed by an asteroid are 74,817,414 to 1. If you find that reassuring, just talk to a dinosaur!

Can you unboil an egg?

Although I am far from a whizz in the kitchen, other than standing in front of the sink, I have always disputed the veracity of the rather pejorative phrase 'couldn't even boil an egg'. My relatively few attempts have resulted in a variable end product. Even more accomplished practitioners of the culinary arts struggle to achieve perfection every time.

The inability to boil an egg consistently rather than the inability to put an egg in a pan of boiling water is no shameful matter. Help is at hand. There is an egg-shaped device now available which you can put in your pan alongside your egg that apparently changes colour to mirror the points between raw and hard-boiled so you can better boil your egg to your taste. I bought one at a car boot sale. The location of my purchase may be a clue as to its efficacy.

But imagine *un*boiling an egg. That, according to the ever popular journal, *ChemBioChem*, is what a team of chemists from the University of California under the leadership of Gregory Weiss have done. From a scientific perspective, when you boil an egg, what you are doing is causing the proteins to unfold and refold into a more disordered and tangled structure. The idea Weiss wanted to test is whether you could reverse the process, changing the proteins from their unruly mess to a more ordered state. And it seems you can.

It is quite simple, but if you can't boil an egg, you may have some difficulty. First you take a hard-boiled egg that has been boiled for twenty minutes at a temperature of ninety degrees Centigrade – now *that* is hard-boiled. Next you add a substance, unspecified in the reports I have read, that strips away the egg white and liquefies it. The remains are then put into a vortex fluid device, specially designed for the purpose by Flinders University, which produces shearing forces that knock the proteins back into their former untangled state. And voilà, your egg is unboiled.

Fascinating as this may be in the abstract, there are actually some anticipated benefits from this discovery. Proteins are tricky devils and have a tendency to fold in unanticipated ways when they are being used in the manufacture of pharmaceuticals, meaning that they cannot be used for the intended purpose. Conventional methods available to straighten them out are both costly and time-consuming. The benefit of the Weiss method is that it is both considerably quicker – a matter of minutes – and likely to be cheaper, thus allowing drug manufacturers to make even more money.

There is one final point to clear up, and that is how this all squares with the second law of thermodynamics, which superior science wallahs often explain to ignoramuses like me by comparing it to cooking eggs. Once you've scrambled an egg, you can't separate the yolk from the white because to do so would create order from disorder.

The second law, as I'm sure you don't need me to tell you, states that the degree of disorder or, as it is technically known, entropy, will always increase in the universe. Weiss's experiment at first blush would tend to stand this rather picturesque metaphor on its head because order is being created out of disorder. But worry not. A by-product of the process is the production of entropy in the form of heat, which offsets the decrease in entropy caused by the fact that by unboiling an egg you have increased order.

Glad we've unscrambled that one.

Do humans have the same range of facial expressions?

A picture is worth a thousand words, they say. Every picture tells a story. The human face can be wonderfully expressive and can give the onlooker a sense of what you are thinking or feeling without the need for you to utter a word. To the enquiring mind, the obvious question is whether there is a stock range of expressions for emotions. Putting it another way, Do humans make the same facial expressions in response to the same emotions?

An interesting question, you might agree, and one that a graduate scientist at the University of Minnesota, one Carney Landis, applied his mind to in 1924. The starting point was to assemble a group of volunteers, most of whom were drawn from Landis's fellow graduate students. His idea was to submit his colleagues to a range of situations that would evoke different emotions, ranging from joy to fear, and examine the facial expressions that each made. To make life easier for himself, he decided to divide the human face into a series of sections following its musculature and to paint lines around each section. By taking a series of photographs, he would be able to determine how each volunteer responded and which part of the face moved in response to any given stimulus.

Having developed the methodology, the experiment began. The key, obviously, was to assemble a range of stimuli that would provoke a strong reaction. So, rather like a Bushtucker Trial, the guinea pigs were asked to put their hands in a bucket of slimy frogs. Whilst this was going on, Landis was happily snapping away. They were asked to look at pornographic images, were subjected to electric shocks, smell ammonia … You get the picture.

All went swimmingly until Landis produced a live white rat on a tray and asked them to decapitate it. Even allowing for the fact that sensibilities around animal rights were not as advanced as they might now be, this bizarre request caused a bit of a stir amongst the volunteers. What was interesting, and perhaps the most significant outcome of the bizarre experiment, although the import seemed to have passed Landis by, was that only a third of the volunteers actually refused to carry out his command. Had he pondered this phenomenon, he would have pre-empted Stanley Milgram's equally disturbing experiments of 1963 that investigated the extent that people would obey orders even if it meant causing others harm. The students' noble refusal to obey Landis didn't spare the rats. Landis did the job for them.

The other two thirds, with some reluctance, set about butchering the rats. The trouble was that the executioner's art is a rather skilled one, calling for a steady hand and steely determination, and most made a bit of a fist of it. According to Landis's notes: 'the effort and attempt to hurry usually resulted in a rather awkward and prolonged job of decapitation'. It is hard to imagine the scene of devastation as the rats suffered a slow and painful death. Perhaps Landis should have concentrated on looking at the expressions on the rodents' faces.

And the result of this rather odd experiment? Try as he could, Landis could not see any correlation between an emotion and expression. It seems that people have a wide range of facial expressions to convey the same emotion. Still, it is good that we have cleared that one up.

Can you fry an egg on a pavement?

'It is so hot outside, you could fry an egg on the pavement'. A curious phrase indeed and one I have always taken as being figurative rather than one grounded in fact. Leaving aside considerations of hygiene – after all, you can never be quite sure what has been on the pavement before – to the enquiring mind the obvious question is whether it is really possible.

The starting point in our investigation is the humble egg. As we have seen, in order to cook, the proteins in an egg need to have their molecular structure modified by a process known as *denaturation*. Then they must coagulate. For the process to start and be maintained to ensure the egg is perfectly cooked, temperatures need to be between 144 and 158 degrees Fahrenheit. This would seem to rule out conducting the experiment in Blighty, where temperatures rarely rise above 100 degrees. Even then, it is so rare that you could be waiting a long time to even attempt the experiment.

The next ingredient in the experiment is the pavement and its characteristics. Here I am indebted to Robert Wolke for some research reported in his book, *What Einstein Told His Cook: Kitchen Science Explained*. Wolke found that temperatures of pavements can vary, depending upon the composition of the pavement, whether it is in direct sunlight, and on the ambient air temperature. Dark pavements consisting of tar or similar materials absorb more light than concrete ones and so would be the pavement of choice. But disappointingly, Wolke found that pavements rarely reach a temperature above 145 degrees, frustratingly just short of the minimum temperature needed to cook an egg.

The next problem is that when you crack an egg and pour its contents onto your pavement of choice, the egg will cool it slightly, and as the pavement is a poor conductor of heat, you will be lucky, without an additional source of heat, to get the temperature back up to a point where the egg will be cooked evenly. The reason we fry an egg in a frying pan is that metal is a good conductor of heat and gets hotter, allowing the optimal temperature to be more easily achieved. If you really want to fry an egg al fresco using the natural power of the sun, then you would be better off using the bonnet of a car. As they say, make sure you have the owner's consent before you try as the mess it leaves may cause offence.

Arizona is a state where temperatures are regularly high and humidity is low. The conditions are such that on July 4th each year – a day when we Brits celebrate the departure of the American colonies from the benevolent British Empire – the good citizens of Oatman hold an annual Solar Egg Frying Contest. As it says on the tin, the contestants have fifteen minutes to fry an egg by harnessing the power of the sun. However, to illustrate and confirm Wolke's findings, they are allowed to use artificial aids such as mirrors, magnifying glasses, and reflectors to aid the process. The lack of humidity also helps because liquids evaporate more quickly and so the eggs dry out faster.

So I suppose the answer to our question is yes, but only with some additional assistance.

How do you spot a liar?

Having worked all my life in the financial services industry, I have come across people from time to time who, to use Alan Clark's delicious phrase, were 'economical with the actualité'. Of course, many take the view that in certain circumstances it is kinder to conceal the truth, to tell a white lie. As Oscar Wilde more eloquently put it: 'a little sincerity is a dangerous thing and a great deal of it is absolutely fatal'. The contrary view is espoused in the lyrics to James Morrison's ditty, 'Broken Strings': 'The truth hurts, and lies worse'.

Wherever you stand on this moral dilemma, it provokes the question, How can you lie convincingly? Conversely, what are the warning signs that suggest that someone is not being entirely truthful?

One route is to strap the other person to a lie detector. In some situations (many, on reflection) this may strike the person you are conversing with as rather extreme behaviour and may engender an atmosphere of distrust that might not have otherwise been there. But the theory behind a lie detector may be of some assistance. The underlying principle is that because telling a porky is an unnatural activity, the body subconsciously sends out signals that are suggestive of an internal struggle.

So here are some warning signs or tips.

There is a tendency to constrict your pupils when lying. If possible, someone who is endeavouring to tell a pack of lies should arrange the seating and lighting so they can see the other person's eyes but not vice versa. The average eye contact time when conversing is 75 per cent of the time spent in conversation. The aspiring fabulist should aim to hit this target. I know this will be hard for accountants and actuaries whose gaze is normally set at shoe level, but then that just might be the point. And don't just stare at the pupils, the fabricator should look at the whole physiog.

The successful liar needs to pay attention to the quality of voice because it has a tendency to go flat when lying. The key to success is controlling pitch and resonance. Someone staring fixedly into your eyes and with a voice going everywhere is likely to be trying to pull your leg. Body posture is another tell-tale sign. Concealing the truth tends to make the body more rigid and solid. To hide your discomfort and say what you have to say whilst maintaining your normal body pattern is difficult, not least because you may not be aware of how people perceive you in normal circumstances.

Another tell-tale sign is blushing. When you feel awkward, your skin gets warmer, and you feel an irritation around your nose and face. The only way to deal with it is to rub or lightly touch the affected area. Excessive hand-to-face contact is a good sign that something is not quite right. It is so automatic a reflex that only the most accomplished fabulist can control it.

Some research from California State University that I came across recently suggested a link between the urge to go to the toilet and the ability to pass off a lie successfully. It is all to do with something called the *inhibitory spillover effect*. You are so concerned about avoiding a spillover effect on your trousers that the body starts to exercise the level of self-control required to control the other tell-tale signs of the deceiver. If you are in a meeting and someone is drinking a prodigious amount of water and then starts squirming, beware is all I can say!

Can a spider's web help diagnose schizophrenia?

One of the most beautiful sights is a spider's web glinting in the sunlight or covered in frost. The patterns that the arachnid weaves are mind-boggling, and I rarely have the heart to disturb them. Of course, if I were a fly, I would have a different perspective. But ignoramus that I am, it has never crossed my mind that a spider's web could be a key to diagnosing schizophrenia.

Fortunately, some people in this world are able to make what to many of us would seem a major leap into the logical void. One such was a Swiss biologist called Hans Pieter Rieder from the Friedmatt Sanatorium and Nursing Home in Basle, who conducted a bizarre series of experiments in the 1950s to further human knowledge.

The starting point, though, was some work carried out by a pharmaceutical researcher, Peter N Witt, in 1948. Witt discovered that spiders, whilst high on drugs, wove markedly different types of web from those that were straight. Quite how he hit on this is anyone's guess, but then we are not scientists. Whilst the cause of schizophrenia is a mystery to this day, healthy patients who have taken drugs such as mescaline or LSD exhibit the same sort of short-term hallucinations and personality disorders as those suffering from schizophrenia. Perhaps schizophrenia was induced by some chemical high generated by the bodies of the sufferers.

Rieder's genius was to link the behaviour of blissed-out spiders and the quest to diagnose schizophrenia. The logic, if indeed it can be so described, was that if spiders were given something from a known schizophrenic and the spiders wove a web of eccentric design, the conclusion must be that they had received a hallucinogenic substance in whatever they had been given. Genius. But what to give them? The answer was as obvious as the nose at the front of your face: *urine!*

So the intrepid Rieder and his team collected fifty litres of urine from fifteen schizophrenics and fed the concentrate to some spiders. The webs they spun were then compared with the webs spun by spiders that were fed with urine from the researchers, the assumption being that none of the researchers were schizoid, a conclusion that must be open to some doubt given the bizarre nature of the experiment. Nonetheless, they persevered, trying different levels of concentration. To say the least, the results were disappointing. Although the webs constructed by the urine-quaffing spiders were different from those created by spiders that had not touched a drop, there was no discernible difference between the webs of spiders who had touched the urine of schizophrenics and those that had drunk the urine of the researchers.

Whilst there may have been a fundamental flaw in their initial assumption, Rieder and his team were forced to conclude that the geometry of a spider's web isn't a reliable clue to the detection of schizophrenia.

But one thing did come from this madcap experiment: Concentrated urine must taste unpleasant to spiders. After taking just one sip, the spiders did everything they could to avoid contact with it again. They would return to their web only after they had given their body parts a good rub and removed all vestiges of the urine. So if you are infested with spiders, don't put a bowl of conkers in the corner of your room, have a wazz. They can't stand the stuff!

How does the digestive system work?

Ever wondered how the human digestive system works? For me, it is sufficient to know that if I put some food in my mouth, masticate it, and swallow, then somehow my stomach will extract what it needs and pass the rest out to be excreted. In the days before X-rays and scanners, the ability to satisfy the desire to know the inner workings of the digestive system was limited.

But for surgeon William Beaumont, now regarded as the father of gastric physiology, fate handed him on a plate a perfect opportunity to understand the workings of the human gut. On 6 June 1822, Alexis St Martin was accidentally shot in the stomach by a discharge from a shotgun, and despite the ministrations of the good doctor, the fistula (hole to you and me) would not heal completely. The unfortunate St Martin was deemed unfit to resume his previous duties and was employed by Beaumont as a handyman.

Sometime in August 1825, Beaumont began to conduct a series of bizarre experiments into digestion, using the stomach and unhealed fistula of his servant. He would tie a bit of food with some string and poke it through the gaping hole in his stomach and then after a few hours, fish it back out to observe how well the morsel had been digested. The doctor also extracted a sample of gastric acid from St Martin's stomach for analysis.

Perhaps unsurprisingly, in September 1825, St Martin fled to Canada, presumably without a piece of string attached to his stomach. But skipping countries was not sufficient to enable St Martin to elude the strange attentions of Beaumont. The handyman was arrested and brought back to the doctor. Unconcerned by the elopement, Beaumont continued to experiment on St Martin, this time concentrating on the gastric acid that he was able to extract from the unfortunate's stomach. The doctor noticed that when he put food into the phial of gastric acid, it was digested.

This was a light bulb moment for Beaumont. He realised that digestion isn't mechanical, the result of muscles in the stomach pounding, squeezing, and mashing the food. Rather it's a chemical process in which the acids in our guts work on the food to extract the nutrients and other forms of goodness the body required.

Revolutionary as this discovery was, Beaumont did not stop there. In early 1831 he carried out another set of experiments on St Martin's stomach. These ranged from observations of the way the stomach digests food to the effects that temperature, exercise, and emotions have on the digestive process. In 1833 Beaumont published his findings in the nattily entitled *Experiments and Observations on the Gastric Juice and the Physiology of Digestion*. It made his name.

Shortly afterwards, Beaumont and St Martin parted company, the latter going back to his home in Quebec, reckoning this was far enough away from the mad scientist. Unbelievably, Beaumont made several attempts to lure him back, but St Martin thought enough was enough. You can't blame him. You wonder why he allowed himself to be subjected to Beaumont's gruesome experiments. Perhaps he was under some form of indentured arrangement with Beaumont or he just felt he owed the doctor a debt of gratitude for saving his life.

Beaumont died in 1853 from injuries sustained when he hit his head slipping on some icy steps whilst visiting a patient. St Martin outlived him by twenty-seven years, having spent some time touring around the States in the company of a charlatan called Bunting as a sort of circus freak. When he died, his family left his body to decompose in the sun and buried it in an unmarked grave, eight feet deep and with rocks in the casket so that the curious would not exhume it.

The thirst for knowledge reveals some strange tales, to be sure.

CURIOUS QUESTION
The forty-fourth

Is yogurt a cure for dandruff?

One of the problems those of us blessed with a reasonable head of hair can encounter is *dandruff*, those scaly bits of loose skin that descend from our scalp and settle like snow on our collar when we comb our hair. I use an anti-dandruff shampoo that boasts a HydraZinc formula which, reassuringly, suggests the user can look forward to up to 100 per cent removal of visible flakes. It always does to set the bar of expectation fairly low, I suppose.

Whilst scientists can split the atom, their understanding of what causes dandruff and what can be done to prevent it is not as advanced as you may think. Perhaps that is why they wear white coats. But our understanding of dandruff may have moved forward apace, if some research conducted by a team led by Menghui Zhang at Shanghai Jiao Tong University and published in the ever popular *Scientific Reports* is to be believed.

Menghui Zhang invited into his lab fifty-nine volunteers aged between 18 and 60, all of whom had washed their hair two days before, and gathered dandruff from eight different areas of their heads. He then divided them into healthy and dandruff groups, depending upon how much visible flaky skin he could detect.

Up until then it had been thought that a genus of fungi called Malassezia was the principal cause of dandruff, attacking the sebum secreted by the sebaceous glands on our scalps, producing oleic acid, which in turn irritates the skin and causes flakes to appear. My anti-dandruff shampoo's revolutionary formula is based on attacking this dandruff-producing fungus. But Menghui Zhang found Malassezia fungi on the scalps of those who were dandruff-free as well as on those who could create a snow storm of their own accord.

Menghui Zhang switched his attention to the bacteria living on our noddles, propionibacteria and staphylococci. He noted that on the healthy heads with little or no dandruff, propionibacteria made up 71 per cent of the scalp bacteria and staphylococci 26 per cent. But on the heads of those with dandruff, propionibacteria made up just 50 of scalp bacteria, whilst staphylococci accounted for 44 per cent.

These two forms of bacteria compete with each other, and where staphylococci start to get the upper hand, dandruff is more likely to appear. Scalp sebum is a particularly good source of food for propionibacteria. Interestingly, Menghui Zhang found that sebum secretions peak between the ages of 15 and 35 and then tail off, whilst those over 40 had more severe dandruff than their younger counterparts. So it may just be that the way to control dandruff on the scalp is to encourage the good bacteria and suppress the bad.

But how can that be done? Frustratingly, this is the next area for Menghui Zhang to look into, but one approach may be to develop an environment on the head in which propionibacteria could be nurtured. At the very least this may well mean some revolutionary new anti-dandruff shampoos.

It just may be that one source could be yogurts that contain the good bacteria. In 2013 scientists discovered that yogurt laced with propionibacteria could help protect the skin from the hospital superbug, Staphylococcus aureus. Perhaps in a few years' time we will be massaging yogurt into our scalps rather than the current so-called anti-dandruff shampoos, which, if Menghui Zhang is right, may not be as effective as they claim to be.

So now we know!

Is there a limit to how long your hair will grow?

Sorting through some boxes the other day, I came across a number of photos of me in my younger days. As was the fashion in the early to mid 1970s, I took to wearing my hair long. A part of me thinks that now that I have released myself from the tyranny of the five-day-a-week working lifestyle, I just might grow my hair long again and perhaps sport a pony tail. This may, of course, be a whim. I haven't gone whole hog yet. And I might get fed up with an untidy barnet before my hair gets to the requisite length.

These musings led me to consider, as you might expect, whether there is a natural and finite length that hair will grow to. It seems there is, and it is all down to genetics and the three phases in the life cycle of your follicles.

The first phase is known as the *anagen*. From the perspective of hair length, this is the most important because it is the phase during which the follicle grows. How long the phase lasts is generally determined by your genetic make-up, but it can be affected by external factors such as stress or a hormonal imbalance. During this phase, which can last anywhere from between two to seven years for the average person, your hair will generally grow at a rate of a centimetre every twenty-eight days. The anagen phase comes to an end by the release of a signal, the cause of which has yet to be determined.

Once the chemical signal has been triggered, your follicle goes into phase two, known as the *catagen* phase. The upshot is that the outer part of the root is shut off from its supply of blood, which it had relied upon for nutrients, and the cells that are produced to stimulate growth. The result is that this phase signals the end of the follicle's growing phase and lasts around three weeks for the average person.

The final phase is known as the *telogen*. This is where the follicle is in what might be best described as a resting state and is effectively dead from the root up. The follicles in this stage are the ones that come out when you comb your hair. If you don't disturb them with a comb or a brush, they will eventually fall out.

Experts estimate that at any point in time, around 85 to 90 per cent of your hair is in the anagen phase with about 1 to 2 per cent in the catagen phase. The rest of the follicles on your head are in the telogen phase and are liable to fall out at any moment.

Of course, these are averages, and the spectrum of outcomes is much wider. Some people have extremely short anagen phases and, as a consequence, find it difficult to grow their hair. Extreme stress can cause the anagen phase to stop prematurely and increase the proportion of your follicles in the telogen phase dramatically, resulting in rapid hair loss. Others have prolonged anagen phases like the Chinese woman Xie Quiping, whose hair, when measured on 8 May 2004, was 18 feet 5.54 inches long!

Cutting your hair doesn't upset the genetic make-up of your follicles. It just means that the follicles have to start all over again!

What are the floating things
I see in my eyes?

As I have got older, I have been noticing a slightly disconcerting phenomenon with my eyesight. It is most pronounced when I am in bright sunlight or when I am staring at a blank or colourless background. My vision contains a host of amoeba-like shapes that move and change appearance constantly. It is quite striking and entertaining in its own right – a bit like looking into a kaleidoscope or having your own in-built lava lamp. But what are they, and are they harmful?

The technical name for these blighters is *muscae volitantes*, Latin for hovering flies, but they are more commonly known as *eye floaters*. They are, I'm afraid, a sign of inexorable Anno Domini.

The *vitreous humour* is a clear gel, made up of water, hyaluronic acid and collagen that fills the space between your retina and eyeball. When you are young, the vitreous humour is thick and like a gel. Unfortunately, as you age, the hyaluronic acid breaks down and releases the trapped water molecules. The consequence of this is that the core of the vitreous humour becomes more watery, and little bits of undissolved gel break off and slowly drift around. The shadows of these pieces are thrown up against your retina, and when light passes through it, you see them as floaters.

Because they follow the movement of your eye, it is difficult to look at them directly. Instead, and somewhat disconcertingly, they will often move to and stay at the periphery of your vision. Many of them will just sink to the bottom of your eyeball. If you want to get a really good look at them, lie down on your back and look at the sky or a featureless ceiling. Some of the floaters will settle around the *fovea*, that area at the back of your eye that is responsible for your central vision. If that happens, you will get a clear view of them. Because they are inside your eyeball, they are not optical illusions but rather entoptic phenomena.

Now that we know what they are, are they anything to worry about? As with everything in life, they are fine in moderation. They are just a sign of growing old. However, if you notice a sudden proliferation of them, particularly in combination with some other form of eye-related issue such as blurriness, flashing lights, or loss of peripheral vision – and these symptoms have not been caused by excess alcohol consumption or over-enthusiastic use of recreational drugs – then that might be a sign of trouble. Sometimes floaters can be symptomatic of the vitreous humour pulling away from the retina or an abnormal growth of blood vessels in the eye. In that case, see the quack pronto.

How do human eggs fertilise?

The purpose of this book is to tease out the answer to those little questions that occasionally trouble us as we travel the journey of life. This question – How do human eggs fertilise? – goes to the root of life itself, and our understanding of the process has been immeasurably improved by a recent discovery reported in the ever popular journal, *Nature*.

As everyone surely knows, part of the mystery was unlocked in 2005 when a team of Japanese researchers identified the sperm protein that they called IZUMO1 after the marriage shrine in the Land of the Rising Sun. It is only now that scientists – Brits, I'm pleased to relate – have identified the other side of the equation, a protein in the form of a molecule that sits on the egg's surface and binds with a male partner on a fertilising sperm cell. Without this binding, fertilisation cannot happen, the men in white coats claim. The molecule has been named Juno after the Roman goddess of fertility.

How was this key to the formation of life discovered? Inevitably it involved mice. What would we do without these furry creatures? Female mice were bred to produce eggs that lacked the Juno molecule. The result was that all of their eggs were incapable of fusing with normal sperm. Then a set of male mice were developed who each lacked the IZUMO1 sperm protein. They, too, were unable to participate in the conception process, emphasising the pivotal role of the protein in male fertility.

It seems that the Juno molecule becomes undetectable some forty minutes after the pairing. Once an egg is fertilised by one sperm cell, it puts up some form of barrier against others, a defence mechanism that prevents fertilisation by more than one sperm, which would lead to an embryo with too many chromosomes.

What this all means is that even with IVF, if the eggs do not contain Juno, then fertilisation will not occur. Despair not if you are embarking on an expensive course of IVF treatment. It is possible to bypass this natural mating of IZUMO1 with Juno by injecting a sperm directly into an egg.

Clearly the discovery opens the way for some interesting applications. Tests for the presence or absence of these proteins may help to establish why one or the other of a couple are having trouble conceiving. At the other end of the scale, the manipulation of the way the Juno protein or its alter ego, IZUMO1, operates could produce an alternative and more effective form of contraceptive.

What is the best way to get rid of hiccups?

I find that an attack of hiccups (or hiccoughs) is an increasingly common aftereffect of a good meal. I don't know whether it is a sad commentary on the state of my digestive system, but there we are. At least for me an attack lasts a minute or so, unlike poor Charles Osborne, who started an attack whilst attempting to weigh a pig before slaughtering it. Despite increasingly frantic attempts to find a cure, he continued hiccupping for a total of sixty-eight years, until February 1990, earning himself, if nothing else, a well-deserved place in the *Guinness Book of Records*. During the first few decades of his affliction, he was hiccupping at a rate of forty times a minute, although he slowed down to twenty a minute in later years. That's the thing about hiccupping: their rhythm, the rate at which you hiccup, tends to be fairly constant during an attack.

A hiccup, or *synchronous diaphragmatic flutter* as the medics snappily call it, is an involuntary contraction of the diaphragm involving a neural pathway called a *reflex arc*. Once triggered, the reflex causes a strong contraction of the diaphragm followed shortly thereafter by closure of the vocal chords, resulting in the telltale 'hic' sound. Fortunately, for most people, socially inconvenient as an attack may be, they are short-lived.

There are many supposed cures to accelerate their departure. I find a series of long deep breaths does the trick for me.

Some of the suggested cures (I cannot attest for their efficacy) are:

- Placing a teaspoonful of sugar on the back of the tongue.
- Sticking your fingers in your ears. Apparently the same vagus nerve that is affected by a hiccup has a branch that goes up to your lughole. (This explains why I have never seen a folk singer succumb to an attack.)
- Gargling with water long enough to interrupt the hiccup cycle.
- Breathing into a paper bag long enough to rid your body of its increasing level of carbon dioxide.
- Placing a paper towel over the top of the glass and then drinking the water through the towel. Apparently the process causes your diaphragm to work harder and should have the effect of restoring its equilibrium.
- Sticking your tongue out to stimulate the vocal cords to open and to allow yourself to breathe more easily.
- Swallowing or sucking on something sour like a teaspoon of vinegar or a lemon.
- Holding the top of a door frame and leaning forward.
- Taking gulps of water in rapid succession.
- Submitting yourself to a scare.
- Engaging in a long, passionate kiss.
- Drinking from the side of the glass furthest away from you – for the contortionists amongst you. This involves holding your head at a peculiar and uncomfortable angle.

Still, having hiccups may not always be a bad thing. In Indian, Nepalese, and Arabic folklore, an attack occurs when you are being thought of by someone close. And according to Slavic, Baltic, and Hungarian custom, hiccups signify that someone who is not present is talking about you.

So now we know!

Why do knuckles crack?

I have to admit it: One of the most irritating things someone can do in my presence is crack knuckles. I long for the moment – it will be delicious when it arrives – when someone dislocates one or more digits in the process. Until then, I will just have to grin and bear it.

A recent exhibition of knuckle cracking in my proximity led me to wonder why this happens and why, alas, the perpetrator is able to put them back without any apparent harm. I was astonished to find, upon reading a report in the ever popular journal *Plos One*, that whilst the phenomenon was acknowledged, the cause had not been the subject of detailed scientific investigation until a team of Canadian scientists under the leadership of Professor Greg Kawchuk from the University of Alberta looked into the topic.

Our story starts way back in 1938, when a German physician called Nordheim demonstrated that most joints in healthy people can be made to pop when pulled – research, I'm sure, the Gestapo made good use of. The *why* he never addressed.

In 1947 a couple of doctors at St Thomas's Hospital in London conducted their own research into the knotty problem. They found a volunteer (there is always one), tied a cord round his fingers, and told him to tug until the joint popped. The docs captured what happened on a series of X-ray images and concluded that a tension of around seven kilograms was required to make the bones in the knuckle separate by about half a centimetre.

As to why this happened, they thought that the cracking occurred when the joint surfaces were wrenched apart, causing a sudden drop in pressure in the synovial fluid around the joint for a bubble to be formed. Gratifyingly, once cracked, the same knuckle wouldn't crack again for around twenty minutes.

For anyone who cared about such things, this was the commonly accepted explanation until in 1971 scientists from Leeds University repeated the St Thomas experiments and concluded that the crack came from the swift collapse of the bubble, not its formation.

And there matters stood until some Canadian scientists came along and videoed, using a MRI scanner, what exactly happens internally when knuckles are cracked. They found that every crack occurred precisely when the joints suddenly separated and a gas-filled pocket appeared in the synovial fluid that lubricates the joint. As the pressure in the fluid drops, a bubble is produced from the gas in the fluid. The natural reaction of the joint is to resist the pulling, but at some point, probably when the tension is some seven kilograms, it will suddenly give way with a crack.

So it seems that the London doctors were right, and one of life's many little mysteries has been solved. Rather desperately trying to find an application for this discovery rather than just glorying in putting a thorny problem to rest, Kawchuk suggests that the regular monitoring of the ability of those who can crack their knuckles will give a clue regarding the health of the joints. Get out of here!

So now we know!

Does the humble carrot make you see better in the dark?

'Eat up your carrots', I was told as a child. 'They will make you see better in the dark.' It was something I swallowed at the time, but now that I am older (if not any wiser), I wonder whether it is an old wives' tale or there really is something to it.

Our pursuit for the truth starts with the dark days of World War II, when Britain was under attack from German bombers, and when the British government instituted blackouts to make the prospective targets for the night-time raiders more difficult to identify. By 1939 the Royal Air Force was prototyping a radar system known as on-board Air Interception Radar (AI) that enabled it to spot enemy aircraft as they crossed the Channel. In 1940 John Cunningham, who was nicknamed 'Cat's Eyes' because he downed nineteen of his twenty kills at night, shot the first enemy plane down using the AI system.

Radar was to have a transforming effect on the fortunes of war. Naturally, the Brits wanted to keep it under wraps but at the same time wanted to raise home morale. So some genius thought that Cunningham's success could be ascribed to his consumption of carrots. An advertising campaign was launched, proclaiming in the stilted style of the time: 'Carrots keep you healthy and help you see in the blackout'. Catchy or what?

This campaign coincided with a glut of carrots at the time, and the government was struggling to find ways to encourage the reluctant public to consume indigenous root crops. Colourful characters such as Doctor Carrot and Potato Pete were introduced in 1941 to aid the campaign. Even Walt Disney got into the act. One of their leading cartoonists, Hank Porter, created a whole family based on the Doctor Carrot idea, consisting of the likes of Carroty George, Pop Carrot, and Clara Carrot.

And it worked. The Ministry of Food in February 1941 was able to report: 'The consumption of carrots has increased following the Ministry's publicity campaign'. Whether the Germans were as gullible is another story.

There is, though, a modicum of truth in the story. Carrots have long been known to be beneficial to the overall health of the eye because of its high vitamin A content. Specifically, vitamin A protects the eyes from night blindness, and not having enough of the orange root vegetable can lead to problems such as dry eye and cataracts. So there is at least a case to make that the carrot helps to keep the eyes healthy, even if they don't imbue you with the power to see at night.

And before we go, one additional carrot factoid. Their original colour was purple. It was only in the seventeenth century that the orange carrot that we are so familiar with started to appear, thanks to the work of Dutch horticulturists, probably in an attempt to get the colouration of the vegetable to match the national flag of the time.

So now we know!

Lightning Source UK Ltd.
Milton Keynes UK
UKOW04f2003041017
310413UK00001B/70/P

9 781546 280026